THE
BLACK
EXPATRIATES

THE
BLACK
EXPATRIATES

A Study of American Negroes in Exile

edited and with an introduction by ERNEST DUNBAR

E. P. DUTTON & CO., INC.
NEW YORK   1968

Library of Congress catalog card number: 67-11363

Published simultaneously in Canada by Clarke,
Irwin & Company Limited, Toronto and Vancouver

First Edition

To Dorothy

Acknowledgments

To all the contributors to this book, who paused in their busy lives and gave me the benefit of their thoughts and experiences, I extend my heartfelt gratitude. I am indebted also to others who provided insights and furnished leads to informative interview subjects. Among these are Robert and Ina King, Dr. Calvin Browne, Stanley Marshall, Sue Yellin, Melvin van Peebles, Colette LaCroix, William Gordon, Ollie Harrington, William Gardner Smith, Frank Scott, Jack Lind, Mr. and Mrs. Nathan Boyd, Dr. and Mrs. J. Gikonyo Kiano, Mattye Iversen, Herbert Gentry, Clive Farel-Boston, Fletcher Martin, Art Simmons, Leroy Haynes, William Davis, Dr. and Mrs. Syoum Gebregziabher and Henrik Wolsgaard-Iversen.

ERNEST DUNBAR

Contents

Introduction

Several years ago I found myself in Moscow on a magazine assignment. While there I bumped into another American Negro, a friend from New York, who was doing postgraduate work in Russian studies. My friend told me of the existence in Moscow of a Negro from Detroit named Robinson who had lived in the Soviet Union for thirty years. The Detroiter had been a Ford Motor Company machinist in the early thirties whom the Russians had brought over on contract to teach his skills to their own workers. He was lionized by the Russian people to whom a Negro then was a rare specimen. After they had renewed Robinson's contract several times, the Russian authorities invited him to become a Soviet citizen. He decided that there was a lot more going for him in Moscow than in Detroit, took out Soviet citizenship and stayed.

My friend and I went to visit him. As we approached the huge, gray complex of Stalinist Modern apartment buildings in which he lived, we became a little bewildered. All of the buildings looked alike and, though we had the address, the numbering was not done in a way with which we were familiar.

As we peered up at the numbers over the doorways, a couple of Soviet citizens came up to us out of the winter gloom, obviously eager to be of help, and asked: "ROB-een-son? ROB-een-son?" We said *"Da,"* and they led us to a building two blocks away, where we finally located our man.

I was struck by the fact that after the passage of thirty years, Robinson's neighbors still assumed that any dark Americans wandering around that vicinity must be looking for *him,* and that even people blocks away knew him. After thirty years and a change of citizenship, he was still an "American."

On my assignments as a magazine writer, I have sometimes run across American Negroes in places where I, at least, would hardly have expected to see them. We exchanged greetings, talked about people or places we knew in America and about the country in which we were at that moment. But since I was on a story which had little to do with *their* story, the pressure of time and events kept me from learning more about their life in a new country. So we parted with a lot unsaid, questions unasked and gaps to be filled in.

The present volume is the result of a trip I finally made to obtain some of the answers I'd not had an opportunity to get before.

If you are not a Negro, you may ask what is so important about the experience of a Negro expatriate. Why should his sojourn in another country have different dimensions than that of the white American living abroad? My answer would be: because he is a Negro. Even *in*

America his experiences, his perception of himself and his country differ radically from what other Americans regard as reality.

Belonging to the group called American Negroes—or Afro-Americans, as many now feel to be the more correct description—bears with it the psychological, cultural and ritualistic trappings of membership in any other fraternal lodge. There is so much that Negroes do not have to say to each other—even Negroes who are total strangers—because it is understood, a web of memory and experience upon which new edifices of thought and language are constantly being erected. So much of this tacit communication occurs between Negroes that to have to go into an explanation for a white friend is sometimes the occasion for dissembling or for what must seem to the white listener to be a patronizing lecture.

There are many reasons for the Afro-American's special view of the world and his place in it, reasons that have been accumulated out of four centuries of living in America, that have been hammered by adversity and annealed in the fires of survival. His view of America has been conditioned by the special nature of his arrival in that land and the special experience he has undergone since that time, an experience shared by no other ethnic group in America.

Out of that background has come a whole culture: a way of talking, an original approach to music, a kind of cooking, a brand of humor that links both regions and generations. At the same time, the Afro-American is *American*— even in a society which would often try to deny him that status—and that fact gives him another view. For his own situation has forced him to see behind the slogans and the glitter to the American reality, the America that is. But the black American must live among and interact with the white American majority, who talk and act as if the America of the brave slogans and plastic flags were real.

For example, he may be sent to Vietnam to die for the "freedom" and safety of Asians at the same time that the U.S. Attorney General confesses to an inquiring Congress and the world that the all-powerful U.S. cannot guarantee the safety of the black American in his own country. His presence in Vietnam itself, in numbers far larger than his proportion in the population, is the result of multiple discriminations of the past and present: of inferior public schools shortchanged by the society, of biased employers and unions which have allied themselves with the educational swindle so that large numbers of Negroes have remained at near-Depression-level income for more than two decades (many retreat into the military which, if nothing else, pays regularly) ; and then that final discrimination, the draft itself, geared to favor the better educated and the well-to-do—both categories from which the society has deflected the Negro—sucks him up and deposits him in the front lines to fight for "democracy."

So the Afro-American is constantly trying to resolve problems of identity, perpetually bound up in his split-level view of the American society and preoccupied with his struggles to establish his own place in that society. For many, the battle for integration is complicated by a rejection of some of the dominant values of white America. The black American is therefore fighting a schizophrenic crusade: to get into the society and to radically alter it, both at the same time!

The Afro-American, then, is a special case, bred and bled in America. But what happens when he is removed from America? Out of the land where he is one of 22 million blacks in a nation ruled by 175 million whites? Out of a land where black and white view each other through prisms of perception colored by guilt, suspicion, bitterness and envy? Out of a nation where elaborate social fictions have been created to paper over deep gulfs and ragged inequities?

The purpose of this book is to answer some of these questions. The people I sought were those who had chosen, for any one of a hundred reasons, to leave the land of their birth and live abroad. They were not employees of the United States Government constrained to make accommodating apologias because of their positions—or employees of firms or foundations who were overseas merely because their jobs had led to their transfer. They are black men and women who, at some point in their lives, decided to leave America to live in another country. Most of them are still American citizens but find life beyond these shores in some way more fulfilling.

The countries in which I sought these black expatriates were chosen for a variety of reasons, all of them pertinent to the special condition of the American Negro. Africa, of course, is an obvious choice. It is a continent to which I have traveled for almost a decade and in which I have discovered Afro-Americans in various stages of adjustment. It is both the continent of our origin and a land of self-discovery. White writers have argued that the Afro-American is a stranger there; black writers have disputed this assertion, claiming a bond that transcends the distance of miles and centuries. But there are many Africas. To some American Negroes the radical Africa of Guinea, Mali or Tanzania may be as restrictive as Albania or the Soviet Union. To others, the bourgeois Africa of Nigeria, the Ivory Coast or Sénégal is as alien a context as Scarsdale, Dearborn or Pacific Palisades.

Is there an affinity between black Africans and black Americans? Do Africans welcome the Afro-American as a long-lost brother returned home? Does color bridge the gap between centuries of differing experiences? Does the African distinguish between the black American and the policies of the United States government, with which both may at times be in disagreement? And what are the reactions of the Afro-American when he becomes a black man in a black society? These are just a few of the questions that arise when the Negro returns to the continent from which his ancestors were taken.

Then there is Europe. Paris, the traditional refuge of American exiles of all colors, has special overtones for the black expatriate. For liberal France is also *pied-noir* France, Malraux's country was also the land of the OAS. Germany is not only festive Munich or academic Heidelberg, but also the nation in which millions of youngsters who are now adults were taught to hate non-Aryans and in which a minority—white—was singled out to die by the millions because of their differentness. Italy is the splendor of Rome and the infamy of the Ethiopian invasion, the warmth of Italian hospitality and the blind fury of Duce's blackshirts. In short, this inquiry also concerns itself with how the black American fits into a society which perhaps takes no special position toward *him* but has a definite— and oppressive—record of behavior toward another ethnic group. Europe is also the continent of the American GI and the white American tourist, both of whom sometimes carry the virus of racism into their new environment along with the potent dollar.

It is Europe which provides the black American with the opportunity to find out something about himself, his real abilities—and shortcomings. After years of coping with negative prejudices in America he may be surprised and pleased to enter countries—in Scandinavia, for example— where the people are predisposed to like him *because* he is a Negro. (He may in time reflect that since some of these admirers are only seeing him as a symbol of oppression and not as an individual, they too are hung up on stereotypes, but, of course, this kind of analysis may seem like foolish quibbling to people who have been the subjects of so much *negative* stereotyping in America.)

Some of the black Americans who move to foreign lands find that the years of conditioning, the defensive maneuvers, the peculiar mechanisms of survival learned in America have proved impossible to discard, even in a society in which they are no longer appropriate. For them, The Problem has become internalized and every white face is still The Man. Most make the adaptation with the facility of a people that has to adapt to endure and, to them, color becomes of secondary importance. One black ex-Chicagoan in Paris put it this way: "I don't get into this Negro 'bag' of 'Is the cat putting me down because I'm a Negro?' If I ask a French chick to go to bed, I don't worry my head if she says yes or no because I'm a spook—that's *her* problem. I came up on the South Side of Chicago and I've had my ass whipped by black people and by white people and it hurt either way. I didn't say to the cat, 'Are you whipping my ass because I'm colored?' If he was whipping my ass, I said 'Ouch!' Then I took care of *him!*"

These interviews are but a portion of those I actually had in order to find out what the texture, the range, the depth of the black expatriate's experience was like. Some of the individuals I questioned were so deeply alienated from the United States that while they were willing to share their insights with me personally, they did not wish to be quoted in a book which would provide "Whitey," i.e., the white man in America, with any information about their present condition. They had left that society, they felt, and wanted nothing more to do with it in any form. Others simply couldn't have cared less about America and things American. Still others had something in their past—or present—which publicity could exacerbate. A few did not want to be part of an anthology based on color, or so they felt, but rather wanted recognition of their individual achievement. I respected this argument though I didn't agree with it. But most of those I sought out agreed to be questioned.

As you will shortly see, the people whom I've interviewed have been quite candid. Some of the statements contain contradictions but the contradictions remain because they illuminate the sometimes contradictory position of the black American in exile. Frequently the inconsistencies occur because the interviewee is actually making up his mind about something as he talks, something that he may not have had to think critically about until that moment. For example, several Negroes in Paris began our discussion by denying that there was a Negro "community" as such there, although many of them kept in informal contact with each other—however infrequent their meetings—and those in need felt they could always get aid from another black expatriate. Many admitted that there *was* a kind of community even though Negroes in Paris did not live in the same places.

Said one Paris-based Negro: "There is no community because Negroes won't even let themselves become conscious of a need to see or talk to other Negroes. The same way Negroes at a northern integrated college in the U.S. used to go to a football game and carefully intersperse themselves all through the crowd. We have all the aspects of a community except the awareness. You don't admit the awareness."

There are also contradictions between the experiences of black expatriates living in the same areas but that, too, is part of the story and the conflicts are presented to you as they were to me. Both may reflect a reality.

A number of people told me they didn't *really* leave America because of conditions there or that they were *really* not "expatriates," but the same people wound up saying they didn't think they could ever live in the U.S. again.

Unfortunately I was not able to include interviews with American Negroes living in Eastern European countries because of the possibility of repercussions, in America and in their country of residence, and because the political conditions of Eastern Europe do not lend themselves to wide-open, free-ranging discussions. From my own travels there in the past and the brief chats I've had with a few Negroes I met there, I suspect the spectrum of their experience is much like that had by those in Western Europe with the important exceptions involving political restrictions. (Although some political restrictions are encountered by black expatriates in Western Europe, too, particularly in France.)

While I have tried to convey exactly the views given to me by each subject, I take the responsibility for any errors that might have crept into this manuscript.

ERNEST DUNBAR

"I am not now, and never will become—at least, not by my own desire—an expatriate. For better or for worse, my ties with my country are too deep, and my concern is too great. But I am an American artist, and I know exactly what Nathaniel Hawthorne meant when he wrote, from England, around 1861, that 'the United States may be fit for many excellent purposes, but they are not fit to live in.' Nearly all American artists have felt this, and for very good reasons; but we have all—usually, anyway—gone home.

"The danger of being an expatriate is that you are very likely to find yourself living, in effect, nowhere. I am not, for example, responsible for Turkish society, and I can have no effect on it. It is not here that my social obligations can be discharged. This means that, as time goes on, the expatriate may find that he has no real or relevant concerns, and no grasp of reality. He is living, really, on the hazards and energies of other people; he has ceased to pay his way. In my case, I've got no choice but to shuttle back and forth between the New World and the Old. I gain something from both places, after all, and possibly I am simply far too proud, consciously, to side-step a danger. The rest must depend on my stamina and my luck."

—JAMES BALDWIN, *in an interview in Istanbul*

AFRICA

Gloria Lindsey:

TANZANIA

Since the experience of the American Negro in Africa depends to no small degree on the type of Negro who goes and the kind of African country in which he takes up residence, so too is the sex of the black expatriate an important factor. In Africa, males play a dominant role in most societies. While there is an increasing shift toward the greater participation of women in the national life of the new states, and political leaders talk a great deal about the necessity for eliminating traditional restrictions on the aspirations of women, the hobbles of custom still encumber most females.

The Afro-American woman thrust into this context, therefore is called upon to make far more of an adjustment than her male counterpart. Just being an American woman means being accustomed to exercising more autonomy, assuming more initiative, speaking out more freely than is thought seemly in many African societies,

25

many Negro women married to Africans have told me. The potential triggers of domestic conflict can be as significant as what to name the baby or as inconsequential as who should put out the garbage.

The black female expatriate learns what the taboos are and then must decide how much of her customary style she will refashion to fit the African milieu, how much of a concession she will make, if any, to African norms while still retaining what is important to her.

The black woman expatriate has certain advantages on her side. She is a foreigner and, as such, can circumvent some of the rules which African women dare not transgress, for Africans make allowances for the peculiarities of Westerners. Moreover, to the prospective African suitor, an American Negro woman is often a highly desirable combination of Western education and the requisite black skin, a valuable helpmeet for a rising member of the African elite. On the debit side of the ledger, however, is the fact that she is without tribal connections, lacking the political and social assets which tribal ties deliver to a husband in a continent where the clan is paramount.

Gloria Lindsey is a small, mahogany-hued woman with snapping dark eyes, an agile brain, and a large amount of contempt for hypocrisy. She wears her hair in the close-clipped style popular with American Negro girls who identify emotionally with Africa and the black mystique. Sometimes she wears an African "costume," too. Southern born, Middle-Western reared, she went to Africa by way of New York City and the University of Edinburgh where she took a degree in African Studies.

Miss Lindsey, who had taught at a school in East Africa, was interviewed in New York shortly after her return to this country. While she was not an "expatriate" at the time, her reflections on two years of living in Tanzania give valuable insights into the situation of the American Negro woman in Africa. After working in New York for a number of months, Gloria Lindsey decided to return to Africa and is now teaching at a college for girls in Uganda.

Gloria Lindsey

In 1962 I was teaching at a high school in Manitoba, Canada, when I got a letter asking if I was interested in going to Africa to teach the next year as part of a project sponsored by Columbia University. I said yes, and I was flown from Canada to Minneapolis to be interviewed and tested. A professor from Columbia came up, did all that, I was accepted and I went. In a way, I would have liked to have gone on my own but the salary was more attractive going with an American organization. I also knew they would bring me back.

I had wanted to go to West Africa. But this opening was for East Africa, and I took it anyway. It was actually the first I had heard of Kenya. I, like everybody else, had heard of Mau Mau, and I associated this with Kenya. I knew little else. I had put in for Jinja, Uganda, because it looked like a nice place on the map. But I was sent to Moshi, Tanzania, instead. And I never regretted it.

I was born in 1940. And I was twenty-two when I went to Africa. Now mind you, in college I had a lot of freedom as far as life was concerned. But I was brought up in a certain way. I was not allowed to date in high school, for example. And when I went to college, of course, my parents *had* to say, "You're on your own." There was nothing else they could say. So it isn't that I didn't know the score. I hadn't a lot of experience but I *thought* I had.

When I got to East Africa one thing impressed me: the

way kids *wanted* to go to school. It was the same way that *I've* always felt about education. But most people that I lived around had not felt that way. But these African kids will do anything to go to school. Another thing, too, was that their culture, a culture that I tried to understand, that I tried to read about and learn about from the people, was so completely different from many things I knew. And yet, not so completely different, you saw, if you began to compare. I found lots of areas of comparison between maybe someone like me who had been born in the South and, say, someone born in East Africa, silly things that some people might feel aren't important. For example, women stay in their houses a lot there as they do in the American South. I remember that as long as my grandmother was living, if one of her daughters gave birth to a baby, that daughter didn't put any water on her hair and didn't get out of the house for about six weeks after her baby was born.

I found comparable things in East Africa. I'm not saying this is a carryover. But it *was* similar to what I had known. It took a while for me to get into the society enough to find all this out.

When I first got there, I lived in a house with Sally, another American teacher who's white and who had been in East Africa for a year. So we got into a little clique with a lot of Americans. Then I found that nobody *African* invited me anywhere. Except one person, the son of the chief in our area. When I began to realize that I didn't know any Africans—this was by December—I had come in August, 1962—I said, "Oh, no!"

When I was dating the chief's son, that fact put off other potential African dates. It was some time before I realized this. That happened to me another time when I was going out with one of the ministers in the government. Nobody came near my house! Then one fellow finally told me:

"I don't come to your place any more." And I said, "Why? Why don't you come around?" He said, "Because you go with one of the big bosses, they can make trouble for me!" Rumors flew thick and fast there. Anybody you went out with, you were going to marry, that was the way *they* looked at things! But after that, Mandy, another American girl, and I made a very diligent effort to learn Swahili. We wanted to learn it not so much from the point of view of the people, but because of the *women*. We felt that if you're talking English to a woman's husband, and he can speak English and she can't, she'll think you are making advances to him. So we thought, "Well, you'll meet Africans socially in bars but they will never invite you into their homes. However, if you can talk to the women, you'll get right in!" So we did.

I was taken in by an English couple who taught me a lot of the Chagga tribe's history. They were British but they were people who genuinely loved Africans in the way that some old-time British did. They began to sort of open my eyes to what was happening. I would say, "So-and-so asked me for a date," and they would say, "Yes, well, you know he's got two wives, don't you?" And, of course, I *didn't* know that! So I began to sort of "get the goods" on everybody, and people knew that I knew.

Does an approach by a married man mean the same thing that it does here? You mean, that the wife can come and make trouble for you? Or the unpleasant connotations? No, it isn't the same thing. For one thing, as you know, a man can have more than one wife, and there are men who are married to tribal wives but deep down in Dar es Salaam, the capital, somewhere, they keep girls. It is no sort of big secret though. Everybody knows it. The wife says, when you translate it into English, that "he's running with that girl," or "he runs with her." He may be living in Dar and his real wife is living in Machani. She's there looking after the coffee growing, the children, and the shamba, or hut, and he'll be down in Dar es Salaam. Even some of the government ministers have tribal wives but keep Chagga girls. The kept girls are always Chagga because they are the prettiest—at least I think they are. Maybe they're not terribly sophisticated but they've got great natural beauty.

One government minister approached *me* but I said, "*Please,* don't trouble my life. I know your wife." He said, "But that doesn't matter." "Oh, yes, Bwana, it does matter," I said. Of course, you must do it in such a way that you don't offend these people. You always know who is married. Many people would like to talk to you and won't because of your education. That was another interesting thing, too: being a girl in East Africa with a university education, an education like the Europeans had, put an awful lot of chaps off, fellows with very big positions but without the equivalent educations. There was one assistant police commander who had been very abrupt with me about parking even though in that place everybody parked where he wanted to. I remember him coming up to me once and telling me, "You shouldn't park here at the corner like this!" He was very rude. Then he became a police commander and he came around asking, "Would you like to go out?" He wanted to marry me. He and his wife were separated and he wanted to put her away—she was not educated—so that he could marry an educated girl. He wanted something to *show!*

He used to say, quite frankly, "But how could I have known five years ago, seven years ago, when I married, that I would be *this* today? When I married, I was a rookie, an ordinary cop working under Europeans. How was I to know that I would be sent to Britain for training? How was I to know I'd be police commander of a region? But I *am,* and I want to do things right!"

There were times when I found it a disadvantage not to have tribal connections. Decidedly so, in East Africa. Mr. and Mrs. Bright, the English couple, were all the family I had. It served, in a sense, but it was not enough. I had to be awfully careful about what I did and where I went. If I had had a family, people who dealt with me would have had to always think about *them,* and it would have been more to my advantage. I could have moved more freely. But because I didn't have, I always had to be very careful. I had to keep one eye on an exit at all times. Not just a physical exit, but some way of keeping myself clear. Because there was no one really to go to bat for me, I felt.

Were there any special expectations of me by white Americans, because I was American? They tried, but I absolutely wouldn't let them. They wanted me to be part of the "bush telegraph." They came to your house to stay, you came to their house to stay. You could go around East Africa and you would never have to stay at a hotel. There was always some teaching assistant stationed somewhere who would put you up. But I refused to do this. I never used their hospitality. I didn't need it because where I was going, my African friends either had me in a hotel or I had one myself or I was living with an African family. The Americans used to say, "Why don't you come and play bridge with us?" So I'd say, "Oh, no, I'm going to so and so's wedding (an African)." I felt you had to make a choice between African and white society.

I realized this almost as soon as I went out there. I felt I was not going to get to know Africans if I was living with white kids. It cut me off. Mandy and I had a very good understanding. She understood this perfectly. There were times when Polk, another white friend, just could not move with me. There were certain parties to which I would be invited and she wouldn't. This was fine with her because she also had African friends, friends that she had met in the BBC Swahili Service in Britain where she had worked. Being a Wasp, she also had friends out there from Harvard and Princeton. So she never felt removed and we cooled it together when we liked. During our holidays she went one way and I another.

Mandy and I occasionally double-dated. I remember the minister of health of Kenya had two brothers who had spent seven years in California. They came down to Dar es Salaam once and invited us up to Nairobi. They did everything proper. The elder sent the younger brother down by bus and he invited us to come up and everything was all arranged. Two American Negro fellows who were working in Tanganyika, but were going to Nairobi, gave us a ride up. They told us, "We'll tell you where our hotel is because we'll see you sooner than you think." We said, "Oh, nonsense, these Kenya boys have done this thing properly."

We used to go up to Nairobi, frequently, to meet people. It's not difficult to meet people here. If you go to the Dar es Salaam Club you meet everybody who's anybody. Being black *in a black society* changes the image you held of yourself. I don't think one can be in such a society without that happening. I also think that one often gets a false sense of importance. Not in the extreme sense, but one's ego can get out of proportion. So many people are worshiping you, so many people think you're important just because of the job that you have, just because you're a teacher, or because of the people you know. I went into the bank one day and there were two Europeans in front of me. The African teller said to them, "Just a moment," and he took *my* check and cashed it and gave me my money.

Another time an Indian teller did the same thing. There were Europeans and Africans waiting and he told them, "Wait a moment. What do you want, Miss Lindsey?" In the post office it was the same thing. And you had to be the right *shade* of color, too. I had never thought about it very much before, but once I got to East Africa I was glad I was not *light*-complexioned. If I were, someone might have taken me for a European. Because I looked like a Chagga, I sort of fitted right into the physical setting, if nothing else. When these clerks waited on me out of turn I felt very guilty because I know what it's like to be shunted aside. I used to live in Georgia and I remember being sent to pay my mother's electric bill and having these old white people come in and be waited on before *me*. So I could imagine what these Europeans must have been feeling. But then I said to myself, "Heck, let *them* feel it for a change!" Every time I'd go in there, I'd just smile at them—not with malice—and think, "Well, it's *my* turn now." But I do think it has made it difficult for me to come back to the States because now I get so annoyed at the least little thing. Some of these slights are probably just bad service, but my first impulse is to become angry and say, "Well, all right, you so and so." I just loved living there and I think I'll probably go back. But I had to come back to the U.S. for a while to see if I could still put up with what a black person must encounter in this society. I never forget that someday I might *have* to come back here—after all, I *am* an American citizen.

In a way coming back to the way things are here worried me. I come from poor parents who are always telling me, "That's the way white people are, you just have to accept it." It's true that's the way they are but, damn it, I'll never accept it. Still I've got to come back and see how messed up I really am.

Sometimes I tell myself: "If you accept it, you might get something, you might get what you want." I felt I had to come back and see . . . I think mostly I have been trying to discover something about Gloria, because I have felt such different things.

James Baldwin has said, "Exile saved my life." Still he comes back, though periodically he feels he has to go again. So do I.

I tell my relatives about their children: "Don't let them go abroad if you want to keep them close"—and they do. They want their children to live next door and just stay in their little town. So I tell them, "Don't let them go because if you do, I'm sure, somehow, they're not going to be the same." *I* am not. I could never be the same again. It might be easier if I could be but then I don't think I ever was the same as the rest of them, anyway; I was never—as they say—"adjusted."

I went to Africa. I had been told that those people live in trees, that they are savages, and that it is better to be here in America under any circumstances than to be over there. This, at a time when a lot of Africans were coming to the U.N. And I saw all these African kids at school, kids that *didn't* have any inferiority complexes. And you look at these people in Africa who have been under colonialism and think, "Why *don't* they have the same problems and feelings and frustrations and aggressions as we have?" And they don't, they just don't.

There was an absence of concern about color in East Africa. A person was European, yes, but that wasn't what mattered. You got a different *look*. A white chap and I went to the store the other day here in New York. It was a boy with whom I used to associate frequently in East

Africa, and people here stared at us as if there were something illicit going on. In East Africa, people might *think* you were sleeping together but the *way* they thought it was a different kind of thing. . . . They didn't antagonize you as they do here. If you're walking through the Columbia University area and you are part of a mixed couple, people look and some eyes say, "Oh, horrible!" and other eyes say, "Oh, it must be good." You can just read it in their eyes as you go through. So the boy with me in the store the other day remarked, "Isn't this very different from East Africa?" In East Africa it was just not a thing that was particularly important. You were never afraid that violence might result because you were with a person of another color.

I knew I was *safe* in East Africa. I never worried about my person in any way. First of all, it might go back to an arrogance: I knew that no person with less education than mine or an ordinary tribal person would dare to touch me unless he was insane. I knew I could go anywhere I wanted to go at any time. It was like being a British-protected person in the old days. I knew I was in some kind of invisible protectorate and everybody else knew it too. I had this feeling that somebody was concerned that nothing unpleasant happened to me and somebody would suffer if I was hurt in any way. I never really had to worry about anything.

I want to go back to Africa. I wouldn't like to admit that I *have* to go back. Because in that sense it means that I'm running away. I might be, mind you, but I don't like to admit that I am. But I know I am going back. I enjoyed living there, I was very happy there, I never missed the U.S. Granted, I sometimes missed Chef Boyardi pizza or collard greens 'cause I love 'em, but I was never homesick. I missed my sister, I wish I could've seen my little niece, but not so much that I came back to stay with them. I would rather be in a position to send for them so they could have a chance to see, too.

You see, I have talked to people, too, from West Africa. They told me about American Negroes who, they said, were disappointed because they tried so very hard to understand Africans there and they just were never accepted. But most of the people who told me this were *whites*. And what they were really trying to say to me was, "See, you'll never be accepted there." I said to them, "It's no worse than in East Africa. A Pari there who has married a Chagga is always referred to as 'that outsider,' 'that Pari foreigner who's come into our tribe.' " No less so. I realized very early in the game that whether I lived in East or in West Africa, I'd never be anything but "that American Negro who married so and so." I'd never want to be anything else. I would be proud if they said, "She speaks Yoruba or Ibo almost as well as we do." That, to me, would be a comment that would give me pride. *And* until I opened my mouth, *people wouldn't know*. People in Kenya thought I was from Uganda, people in Uganda thought I was from Kenya until I told them. I spoke Swahili. I found the people in Uganda much like certain middle-class Negroes from a Southern American town.

If I'd married an African, could I have tolerated it if he also took other wives? I think, had it been a person I once had in mind, I would have raised as much hell as I dared, and if it hadn't worked, I think I would have kept quiet about it for a while. Again, this is very much *me!* It sort of depends on where you put the stuff at, how obvious it is. Because I don't see too much difference between Africans and American Negro men—or American *men* period. One has *his* mistress across town and the other just has *his* in the same compound. There's not a hell of a lot of difference.

Living abroad has made one change in me as far as coming back to the U.S. is concerned. I absolutely would not be able to come back to America and take any crap. Before, there were so many injustices that one took for granted or didn't even see, because these things had been there so long. But it goes even deeper than that, now that one *can* see. It just permeates the whole structure. Outside of America, there's time to reflect on what happens here and to look back to reinterpret situations that you are not in when you're abroad. There were the sort of things one used to ignore, because they weren't the most important things. Now *all* of them count! I can't ignore any of them. We used to try to fool ourselves, a bunch of us white and Negro kids, when we were in college, that we were all Joe College and that we were palsy-walsy, that there was no racial problem. There weren't any explicit strata, but you just were never asked to their homes if you were black. In Africa I met some white American kids, the nicest people, and I told them there, "When you go home things will be different. *You* may have changed but the people at home haven't changed and they, the society, will make you give in."

Africa changed my attitude about one thing—I don't try any more to be anything but what I am. There used to be a time when I wouldn't eat watermelon in a public place. Now I take it anywhere I can get it. I'm not being defiant or anything. I just feel that if Africans can eat their *couscous* and if Greeks can come and eat whatever they want to eat, let me eat my chitlins and watermelon wherever I want to.

Coming to New York on a bus recently I got dirty stares from other Negroes because I had this big piece of watermelon. And yet I knew *they* wanted some! We stopped at a Howard Johnson's and I sat there and chomped away. The "brothers" were not pleased about it at all, but later some of them looked at me as if to say, "go on, I don't blame you, but I'm just not doing it." Well, Africa has done that for me.

So you see, I just won't let my life be troubled. But I think one shouldn't have to say, "I won't let my life be troubled" every day.

Tom Feelings:

GHANA

Many Negroes leave America merely because they want to see something of life in the rest of the world; that is, for the same reason many whites go abroad. But others depart because each day upon these shores becomes just too much of a struggle, requiring enormous energies simply to cope with the peculiar pressures that beset black folk here. Because he must contend with these daily irrelevancies, the black artist is often left with little to pour into his creations. To at least one such artist, illustrator Tom Feelings, the decision to leave was also bound up in the need to discover whether he possessed real talent and to pinpoint what his artistic shortcomings were, evaluations he felt could only be made outside of America and the kind of factors which, in the U.S., determine success for a Negro.

Tom Feelings is a young man who moves in the hip worlds of Harlem and Brooklyn's Bedford-Stuyvesant *ghetto. He enjoys modern jazz, a good laugh, and the company of the fine young women of those precincts. Feelings, by his own estimate, is no ideologue. When he decided to leave the U.S., he chose Ghana because he felt that country knew where it was going and he approved of its goals.*

I first met Feelings when he illustrated a magazine article I wrote on the condition of the Negro in America. He'd shown me a sheaf of drawings he'd done on people in the South, innocent faces of children and the bottomless masks of their elders. "There's so much to be drawn down there," he remarked to me in wonder. But the sensitive pictures he drew had a limited market in the mass media and Feelings' sense of alienation wore heavily upon him even then.

I next encountered him in Ghana where he had come to fashion a different kind of existence: a black artist in a black state, where art was deemed a handmaiden of politics and national policy. There were new freedoms—and another kind of adjustment.

Tom Feelings

Q: *Did you come to Ghana with the intention of making this your permanent home?*

I wasn't sure whether I would be able to stay so I saved enough money to go back in case things in Ghana didn't work out. I came here from New York City where I was born. Actually Brooklyn is where I lived. I went to Brooklyn's Westinghouse Vocational High School and after graduating from there went on to the School of Visual Arts as a scholarship student to study cartooning. I worked as a comic book illustrator for two years before going into the service.

Q: *Were you sent overseas?*

Yes, I was stationed in Europe from 1954 to 1957. I remember visiting London and being bombarded with a lot of questions about racial problems in America. During the time I was there, the West Indians were coming in and taking the jobs that the British didn't want to take—on the subways and buses, for example. They were also moving into an Englishman's rooming house and then later buying that house—something the English who lived in some of those rooming houses couldn't do—and that's how a lot of race trouble started. As soon as the British got over two thousand or so spooks living in their country, they began to think they had a problem! Now both political parties have adopted an attitude of seeing who can be the toughest on colored immigrants.

I became engaged to an English chick while I was there, but I decided against marrying her when I got back to the States because, along with all the racism I encountered there, I just couldn't continue to go through all those questions that she was always asking such as, "Why do they treat you so bad?" and "Why do they lynch Negroes?" and questions like that!

Q: *Did you find it hard to fit into American life after your period overseas in the military?*

At times. I went back to the same school, the School of Visual Arts, only this time I concentrated on illustration. I hadn't been interested in that before, but illustration had changed during the years when I was in the service. It had become more concentrated on feeling than on realism and that made it more attractive to me. I remember once before I went into the service, I did a comic strip on a lynching. The teacher didn't comment on it directly to me

but told the class, "You shouldn't get your personal feelings into a comic strip." So when I returned to school I
had decided that I was through with comic strips because
what I was concerned about *was* my personal feelings and
what *I* was doing. This time I went into the illustration
class. Every year they would have an exhibition and, man,
I would let everything out of me! Sometimes I wouldn't do
what the school assigned me to do but would draw my
inspiration from what was going on in the country at the
time. Things that I'd read about in the newspapers and be
bugged about I'd let out onto that paper, like a head of a
Negro boy walking in front of a white crowd and people in
the mob holding up signs saying, "Go home, nigger." I
painted it with everything I could get out of me. But I was
rationalizing. I was thinking, "I'm doing this now because
when I get out of school I won't be able to do it."

When I graduated from art school I decided I didn't
want to go into a studio, so I began to free-lance. I thought
I'd try it for a year but things were very rough. Each year
just about the time I was ready to give up, I'd get a job
that would give me enough money to get through the next
year. But the last year before I came over here I became
really fed up. Man, every time I went into an office to see
an art director, he'd look at my portfolios and then ask me
questions which had nothing to do with the work I was
submitting. Questions such as, "Why do Negroes want to
do this?" or "Why do Negroes want to do that?"

I got tired of trying to explain something to people who
really didn't understand *anything*. They would spend all
the time of my appointment asking me about things involving race that they'd read about in the papers that day!
They weren't asking me anything about *art!*

I went to a white agent and he said, "I can't use any of
your work here because we don't handle Negro subject

matter, but there's a Negro photographer here who's thinking of starting a new Negro magazine and he might be able to use your work." The colored cat came in and looked at my stuff, then asked me: "Why are you always drawing Negroes in poverty?" I said, "Man, these drawings are done from *life!*" He told me, "I think you need to see a psychiatrist." Man, *that* was the end!

Q: *So—after you'd gotten out of art school and had been abroad in the service, is that when the problems of race and identity began to bore in on you?*

Yes. I went down South on a magazine assignment and did a number of drawings on Negro kids there. I thought the Negro children in New Orleans were so beautiful, with handsome coloring, but when I came back to Brooklyn I looked outside my own door and saw the same faces. And I hadn't done many drawings of *them.* So I decided that summer to draw the children that I had seen all my life, and that's where I spent most of my time—drawing. I stopped doing things based on what I'd read and been stirred up about in the newspapers and became concerned about what I saw in my own neighborhood. I drew about that instead, the children of the ghetto. Then people started calling me a "children's artist." It's funny how the minute you start to do anything, people try to put a label on it.

Q: *At a certain point, one sometimes sort of turns a corner in his life. Was there something specific that made you decide you had to leave the American scene?*

Sort of. I ran around with a number of different groups in Harlem, all of them trying to deal in some way with The Problem. One of my very close friends is a Negro cat who went to Visual Arts also and who belonged to many of the groups I did. I began seeing something in him that disturbed me. That cat was getting so negative, he couldn't do any positive work. If he came to Ghana, for example, he couldn't work here unless he could criticize somebody here. Not that he would have wanted to come here—but that is what he was like.

I saw all this in him and sometimes I thought I saw it in myself. I'd get in a corner and wonder, "What the hell is happening to me?" I would see things in magazines done by white illustrators on *Negro subject matter,* purchased by the same art directors I'd just been to see, and who'd turned my stuff down. I began to speculate, "Well, maybe they gave the job to this white cat because he's better than I am. But I will never be able to tell *here.* What I have to do is go someplace where I *can* tell."

There was a white guy in my class at art school who used to bug hell out of me. He drew Negro subject matter all the time and had a special portfolio of this work which he carried around to all the agencies when he got out of school. He was doing everything I had been doing and he sold a lot. Almost everything on the subject which was published, he had done. I was constantly asking myself whether I disliked what he was doing because I disapproved of his technique or if it was because he was getting the work. One thing in particular bugged me about his work: he used models and no matter how many different kinds of Negroes he drew, they all became long, tall, slender Negroes, who looked as if they just about had some clothes on. When I complained about this to a number of people, they said, "Aw, you're just jealous of this cat!"

I asked him once why he wanted to draw Negroes and he said, "Just because you're a Negro doesn't mean you can draw Negroes better than me!" I laugh about it now but I didn't laugh about it then. It used to really bug me. But you know, I haven't worried about that guy since I've been here.

Q: *But what was the crucial point at which you decided to leave?*

In the last six months before I left, I was practically going out of my head. Everything I read about in the newspapers—on race—would bug me. And I was a free-lance! If I was going out of my head, I can imagine how the Negroes felt who had to go to an office every day, sitting there seeing these things happening and yet not being able to discuss them with their fellow workers. Or knowing that the white people there *didn't want* to discuss them and would talk about something completely different. I saw this sort of thing happening to a couple of friends of mine. One of them is a bank clerk and I just got a letter from him in which he says he's bought a forty-five. He says he is not going into the service, that he will die right there on his steps, and he means it!

Q: *In short, you felt the pressure of race in America was unbearable?*

I have been told I'm overly sensitive but I guess an artist has a license to be overly sensitive. Anyway, I left. I didn't know whether I was coming back in a month or two if I didn't get a job. But as soon as I got here and took a look at some of these black faces, I thought: "Well, I'll be around here for a little while anyway." Until I got my present job on this Ghanaian magazine, I just walked around and made drawings for a show I gave here.

Q: *Are you able to live on a fairly comfortable scale here?*

I haven't been able to save any money. I eat at the YMCA cafeteria, along with a small group of other expatriates. Sort of a mixed group. The thing I find most relaxing is that we can say what we want and we can say it *loud*. You'll find that Afro-Americans here are loud—not the kind of loudness that Americans exhibit when they go to Europe, but a kind of openness that we often didn't have at home because we were worried about what somebody might think. I'm really not so aware of white people *as white people* any more and I don't have to worry about what I say around them. I can say "nigger" without first looking around to see who's within earshot.

Q: *Is that a tremendous burden off your back?*

Yes. We get over here and we laugh and talk without any inhibitions because whites—American or otherwise—might be near.

Q: *Have you spent any time with white Americans here since this shift in your own attitude?*

I wanted to find out how I felt about whites since I'd left America, so when I met two girls from the Peace Corps at a bar recently and they asked me if I would come over to the Peace Corps house with them, I went. There were other Peace Corps people there, almost all of them young people. They began giving me that line about there being discrimination in all societies and all that jazz. And, of course, asking me about how I felt being here. I was aware of one thing: these people seemed stupid and silly to me, man. Here were young guys who were going back to the States —of draft age—and they were *kidding* about the Vietnam war! I came away from there thinking, "Is this the kind of person I had to put up with in the States?" but mostly I thought, "I'm glad I'm here."

Actually I don't meet that many white Americans. There's one Afro-American here, named Leslie Lacy, attending the university and he meets more white Americans and Canadians. Leslie is an intellectual and this is what he feels he has to do to continue his education. He says: "Man, I have to talk to people whom I can *talk* to." I don't need this, but he does need it. Yet even he gets bugged by what such people sometimes say. He had a Canadian couple over to his house and the Canadians were coming on with the same kind of stupid remarks about "Why do you people—Negroes—keep pushing so hard?" Fortunately I don't run into that kind of person much here. I meet English people over at the "Y" and they sit down at our table, but you can be just as relaxed as if they were not there. We say whatever it is we want to say.

Q: *Do people here spot you right away as a foreigner? Take girls, for instance. You're a bachelor; do you find it difficult to relate to them?*

On the street, people come up to me and start speaking in the Ga language: they think I'm Ghanaian. The business with girls is interesting. I've been going out with a lot of different chicks because I wanted to find out what the girls here were like, but a girl in my office gave me a little warning. She said: "You can't do that here—go out with a lot of women. If you go out with six women in six weeks and other women see you with them, they'll consider you as having six women. There's no such thing as 'dating' here. You go out with one woman. You can have six other women if you like, but you don't take them out. If you do take them all out, not only the women but the men as well will talk about you, saying that you are 'crazy about women.' "

Once I was in a taxi with a girl I was taking to a party and the taxi picked up another girl en route—taxis pick up several fares on one trip in Ghana. The newcomer began talking to my girl in Ga and when we got to the party my girl began acting very strange. When I asked her why, she said the girl in the taxi had told her, "Do you know you are with the most notorious woman-chaser in town?"

Q: *You have said that you have little concern for politics. Isn't that a difficult attitude to maintain here since Africans seem to eat, sleep and drink politics?*

It's true we're surrounded by politics here and I watch what's going on—both here and in the States—as much as I can, but I'm really not political. That's just a fact. I mean, there are cats here who have studied socialism and Marx but I haven't. I just came to do some art work. If I can help the African revolution, all right, but what I'm more concerned with is seeing that some black children will get the type of education they should get. Now I've heard a whole lot of criticism about Nkrumah's acting as if he were a god and I know some of the people who worked around him say he did act that way. But to me, to see a black kid look up to a black man—well, he might as well be a god because I've seen them in America looking up to people to whom they cannot relate at all!

It's true they put up all these monuments to Nkrumah and some of that irked me—probably because I come from America—more than it irked the Ghanaian, but man, I guess you can get to like having people kiss your ass every day. Besides, who are we, as American Negroes, to criticize? We've never been close enough to the big power in the United States to know what's going on—Lyndon Johnson might do a whole lot of eccentric things himself!

I'm probably one of the few black people who actually wanted Goldwater to win, so that a lot of people could see exactly what the real nature of American society is. I'm still concerned about what's happening in the States, but I'm not thinking about coming back right now and being the token Negro who gets all the work dealing with Negro subject matter, or with sitting up in my big office worrying about when some other young black cat is going to come along and pull me off that token slot. No, I'm not concerned about that. What I'm preoccupied with is getting some work done, which is not the easiest thing to do here. Working for the government is like being in the Army: a lot of cats work very hard at getting out of work!

Q: *Are there many Afro-American women here?*

There are four or five of them around. Expatriate women have a harder time here because of the way African men treat women. In some cases, African men may show a greater preference for the Afro-American woman, but she can still encounter problems. The black American chicks come here sometimes because they are looking for what they consider a "black man." But the problem is that even in the States they don't know what a "black man" is supposed to be. It seems to me that what they really want is someone who has a nice job, who is well-to-do and can take care of them, a man who is able to persuade and influence a lot of people and who's *controlling* something. There aren't very many black men in the U.S. who control *anything!* On top of all those qualifications, they want "a guy who's militant"! Now, *that's* a problem! Because most of the guys who have anything are busy just trying to hold on to whatever they've got going for them.

Q: *Is there a close-knit Negro community here?*

There are all kinds of Afro-Americans here, but there is really no Afro-American "community." There are some Afro-Americans here I have not met, and maybe it's better that way. But we do see each other from time to time and if you're in trouble we'll help you out. Like right now there's one young fellow at the university here who's failed, flunked out; we'll get him on a boat somehow and get him back to the States.

Q: *Is there anything about the States that you miss here?*

I miss Southern cooking, although a couple of the Afro-American girls make some "soul" dishes for me every once in a while. I also miss seeing a lot of art work, illustrations, the kind of new things that you are always seeing in the magazines you pick up in the States.

Q: *You've said you've discovered that some of the*

Ghanaians in positions of trust shirk work or may even be siphoning off public funds. This is not peculiar to Ghana or to Africa, but what effect does it have on your personal commitment?

I think every guy who came here on his own, as I did, wants to see what is happening here work. So we get angry when we see any of these local cats *stealing!* It really bugs us. Some of us sacrificed to come here so the thought of these guys stealing every day is too much. But I suppose that is a phase they'll have to pass through. I feel the country's real hope is the younger people who are being trained right here in the country, are aware of the fact that they are *African,* and will work to strengthen Africa and Ghana.

Q: *If you had it to do over, would you still come?*

Yes. Every now and then I get a letter from some of my friends back in the States and I get some idea of the things they are going through. One of them recently wrote me that in the young black nationalist groups, the males and females take out their frustrations on each other. I know something about that myself.

We Afro-Americans here may talk about some of the things some African leaders do when we are among ourselves but I have the feeling that if things don't work here . . . well, I don't know where they will. Ghana is one of the few places that I know of where the racial thing is absent, even interracial couples can relax here, man. And that's something marvelous. If Americans want to see integration really working, they should come to Ghana.

Priscilla Stevens Kruize:

GHANA

*Since the appearance of the newly independent
black African states on the world stage, a certain type of
Negro has evolved in America's black ghettoes. He identi-
fies with Africa and things African and although he has
never set foot upon the continent, he may affect the furry
"Sekou Touré cap" worn by Guinea's President or even
the flowing, toga-like agbada, a costume native to West
Africa. For the female of the genre, an absence of any
make-up may be combined with the close-clipped au natu-
rel hair style patterned after that worn by women in some
African tribes. Some neo-Africans have changed their first
names from Roosevelt or Augustus to the more African-
sounding "Hassan" or "Malik"; in Harlem and Watts
black schoolchildren now answer to the names "Kwame"
and "Kenyatta."*

*The neo-African movement is often a reaching out for
ties to the positive (if sometimes idealized) status of Africa
to replace the negative image of himself given the Ameri-*

51

can Negro by biased history texts, motion pictures and news media. The movement is also an affirmation of blackness, a demonstration that the Negro is no longer ashamed but proud of his color and his forebears. Some of the neo-Africans study the history and cultures of the continent, others are content merely with the theatrics of hairdo or exotic costume. A few manage to make the journey to Africa itself, there to experience what had been, up to that moment, an uncertain dream.

Priscilla Stevens Kruize, twenty-seven, is one of the few. She had been active in the civil rights movement and had taken part in demonstrations in the North as well as the South. After a short visit to Ghana in 1963, she returned to America. But in 1964 she decided to leave the U.S. permanently, and she left for Ghana aboard one of that country's Black Star Line ships. On the voyage she met one of the ship's officers, Mun Kruize, a Dutch national, and they were subsequently married.

In America, Priscilla Stevens Kruize had many African friends and often wore African dress herself. In New York it made her stand out. In Accra, Ghana, where she now lives, she seldom wears African dress because with her short haircut and dark skin she is sometimes mistaken for a Ghanaian, which means being treated like everyone else instead of with the deference accorded the foreigner. She is aware of the inconsistencies in her behavior, but they are part of the problems of identity which she is still trying to resolve.

Priscilla Stevens Kruize

Q: Did the Ghana government pay your way over here from the States?

Oh, no, I managed on my own. It's my second time. When I came the first time—well, you know when you come to a country for the first time, for at least a month you just see the surface of things. You have to really live in a country to see what it's all about. I went to all the leading schools the first time I came, looked at curricula, talked to people in education, and I got the impression that their ideas about early childhood education were the same as mine.

At least the people who were interested in good schools and different methods of education seemed to think my way.

So I came back to Ghana and applied to the Ministry of Education for a position. I thought that before I branched out with a program I should get to know the people, work with them for a year, and this is what I set out to do. But while I was working in the schools, so many things were revealed to me that I didn't know before, things that affect what I can really hope to accomplish here.

Q: *Do you really mean in the* schools *or do you mean in the society itself?*

In the schools *and* teaching the students, just going around to different groups and schools in our community. For instance, early childhood education is not thought of here as being anything of importance now—yet I believe this is something far-reaching. Ghana is a country that is so desperate for teachers that it has to take students from junior high schools and high schools to teach in the primary schools. They call them "pupil-teachers." So, with this kind of emergency educational program, if you can call it a program, you just can't expect the government to spend any money on the kind of thing I want to do. And the people who *can* spend money, that is, the well-to-do and others who have reached a certain income level, are only willing to spend it for *their* segment of society. They want a school for *their* particular group. These children go to boarding school, private schools. No one has really taken the initiative to provide this kind of quality school for the children of the workingman. The government has, of course, built many new school *buildings* but it's the program I'm talking about. In order to have students who understand what you are trying to give them they must first have had a good academic background. If you build a house, the foundation has to be good. This is my biggest frustration: students like those I am now teaching at the training college who don't understand me because their academic foundation isn't sufficient. And it's not sufficient because you have people teaching them who are not qualified to teach.

But people in an underdeveloped country want immediate results, so they spend more on secondary education. My argument is that early childhood education, though it doesn't bring immediately visible results, is the important thing in the long run.

I started an experimental nursery school in my own building—using our garage. People got to know about it and I had seven two-year-olds. Once I gave the parents a questionnaire asking them what they thought a nursery school was, what they thought I was trying to do, and what they thought their children were getting out of my program. I don't like to generalize but the replies I got from these parents—and these were quite the elite of the society —shocked me. They said the children were coming "to play," . . . "to relax," things you wouldn't expect people of their education to say. They never saw that their children had grown intellectually or what was really going on here. If they saw their child planting a seed, they thought they were just playing in the mud, they didn't see that concepts were being built.

55 *Priscilla Stevens Kruize*

Q: *Was there a problem with the government about setting up the school?*

No, because, you see, I didn't charge the parents. I wasn't interested in making money, I was interested in getting some results. Getting the children to grow, getting the parents to get insight into what was going on, how wonderful this kind of approach is and how different their children were, because of this kind of experience. But the only thing that came out of this were complaints such as, "Oh, I don't want my child to go to school with the Stewarts' child" and this kind of status nonsense, instead of, "Oh, isn't it interesting that my child is doing this now," or observing that "he's caught on to this." There was a lot that they could've gotten out of it that they didn't.

My students now at the Teacher Training College are as old as I am and they're from all over the country. I teach education to college students at a two-year training college. The students are teachers who have gone back to college to get a certificate.

Q: *Do tribal differences ever come up in class?*

Yes, they come up occasionally, but not seriously. In the class where I noticed it, they occasionally discriminate among themselves. The Ashanti people have the feeling that they are better than any other Ghanaians. If a girl in one group is reading something about how great her tribe was, a girl from another group will get into an argument or discussion about it. It happens sometimes when they write papers too, but, normally, I think they push tribal feelings a great deal into the background.

Q: *What about getting across what you want to teach?*

It's a problem because, you see, I'm not only teaching them child development and educational psychology but English as well. Many of the students didn't understand my speech, which is probably my own fault, too. I think I made a mistake young teachers often make. We get out of a practice school and start lecturing where we left off in practice school, which is not the way you do it, you see. Also I just took it for granted that my students were more educated than they were. It's frustrating. You know by the questions they ask and the kind of things they contribute in class that they are thinking in their own language and then talking it out in English. It's not easy for some. I think I also talked too fast. And I spoke "American English." But even when they understood my English, the results were about the same.

Q: *Did you come to Ghana with a job lined up?*

No, I didn't have a job when I came. I got it about a week after I came. I don't believe in saving money and so I took a month's salary and, with the help of some of my friends, I just came. That's how I met my husband, on the boat I came here on. He works for The Black Star Line, Ghana's ship line.

The accommodations here in Ghana are marvelous. The average person here—foreigner, that is—lives, I think it's safe to say, better than in many other places.

Q: *Who lives around you?*

I have English people in front of me and an Englishman on the side and a Ghanaian woman up front. We're all mixed up. English, Canadians, Indians, Ghanaians.

Q: *Are you very much in contact with Ghanaians socially?*

Oh, yes. Until recently I didn't have any other friends except Ghanaians. I didn't come here to meet *Americans!* I was really wrapped up in Ghanaian culture before I came. I was more Ghanaian than I was American at home and I am here, too. But in America, I knew Ghanaians with the same interests as mine. I really didn't get to know

Ghanaians in the market—the ordinary people—here because of the language problem, but they got to know *me*.
There were only two of us in the town where I live and I
ride a bicycle; I went to classes on my bicycle rather than
in a car like all the other people. You know, that made me
"different." It's considered odd for women in Ghana. They
all wondered why I didn't have a car. They knew I was
making the highest salary in my department and since
everyone else had a car they couldn't understand why *I* was
riding around on my bike. They all thought I was saving
my money for something fantastic or that I wanted to
"clean up" financially and go home, that sort of thing.

Q: *Have you any close friends among Ghanaians?*

Yes, most of my friends are Ghanaians. We call each
other "brother" and "sister."

Q: *Do they still regard you as an American?*

Oh, yes. It's rather interesting because before I came
here I thought that I would be accepted. This is something
that I thought because, in America, all of the Ghanaians
that I knew accepted me as one of them and I just assumed
it would be the same here. But it isn't like that at all.
There's Betty, this Ghanaian friend of mine. I certainly
know *she's* Ghanaian and she makes *me* feel very American, although I certainly never wanted to feel American.
She doesn't consciously do it, for she's very Western in a
sense, but still every now and then I know. But again,
paradoxically, she was so much like me in so many ways
that I didn't feel that I was learning anything Ghanaian
from her.

As I said, I came here very wrapped up in the Ghanaian
culture. And I wanted to be with someone who, I could
really feel, was part of that culture. Betty is as Western as I
am so I feel that I haven't learned anything from her. But
Susan, my other close friend here, is very Ghanaian. It's

strange but I never felt like an American until I came to Africa. Maybe it's because . . . well . . . my mother says if a soldier's on the battlefront he can't expect to feel safe, and I guess that's why I just never felt like that in America. I was never *called* an "American" till I came over here. The thing is, I fight for the right to come abroad without having to have the stigma of "running away." And yet each time I say something, it sounds like that, even to myself, because I've read about so many Afro-Americans who've come abroad and end up saying something, not directly, but something that *sounds* like they're running away. I wanted to come abroad and live the way I wanted to without the idea of running away. I would love to have the feeling of "Oh, well, that country's marvelous, I'll just go and live there." *Any* country, just because you think the country itself is marvelous. Not because of some experiences you've had somewhere else, that drive you some place, or because of something you need. I have this theory that when you are surrounded by white and there's one speck of black and all the white is saying to you "you're not good," even if you believe, yourself, that you're good, eventually, because you are surrounded by the negative, you will break down and believe it. So to balance this you have to go to a place that's all black, that builds you up, that's the opposite, that gives you equilibrium. I think this is what the American Negro needs to do who is so emotionally involved in his problems that he can't do anything constructive until he reaches this kind of level, this balance. Then you don't go to one extreme or the other; I've gone to the extreme several times. The first time I came to Africa, in May, I had had an operation. In June I was jailed in America and the operation was inflamed again. In the last part of June I was beaten in public by a captain of the police force . . . *in public* . . . in Florida.

Because I was protesting segregation and taking part in a swim-in demonstration. I didn't mind white people being against the demonstration, but my faith just turned when I saw that this brutal beating could be done in public, with lots of people around and nobody would protest. You feel that in a group of people there might be one who might, that there's always something good in the group. At least this is what we hold on to, that there is always something good in life. The climax of the whole thing came when I was being beaten, publicly, by this police captain, in front of these groups of white people who were looking at this in broad daylight, and this one woman looked at me and smiled. I thought, "This woman will help me, I can feel it." It was a real sincere kind of smile, not a smile of deceit or anything like that. And then when we get to court, this same woman smiles again, but doesn't say anything! It seemed to me that there wasn't any hope then. How could this happen? Everything in life goes into these particular incidents. The group, the smiles, the brutality . . . so when I came to that time, I didn't know what to do.

Somehow one always tries to put the pieces back together and someone comes along and builds you back up again. But it gets worse each time you have a fall. The second time I met a crisis was when I was trying to build faith not only in America, but in mankind itself . . . that people were basically decent. The world was in such a turmoil I found it hard to believe that people were ever really *going* to blend together and have some harmony or respect people of different races. And then I got a real jolt: An African friend that I really respected and thought shared this kind of feeling said to me: "You know, no matter how educated you become, people of different cultures can never come together." This was said to me by an African, from Ethiopia! Here was a person from a different culture who, I had thought, had beliefs similar to mine, and then suddenly he comes out with a thing like that. It was as if your mother had turned into your father right before your eyes! It kind of shocks you.

Q: *Did this incident with the police captain take place before you had ever been to Ghana?*

Yes, I left several weeks afterward for my first visit here. I was very anti-American when I came to Ghana the first time. But here, again, I sort of found myself. Then when I returned to America I had another bad experience, and that decided things for me. On the twenty-second of April, 1964, the World's Fair opened in New York and I was a member of the civil rights group that picketed the Florida pavilion. I was arrested with that group and we were taken to the Queens, New York, jail and were kept there for—I don't know how long. We of course all had seen the stories that have been written about the Woman's Detention Home in Greenwich Village. There were about four hundred women that were arrested and of course none of us wanted to go there; we'd rather have faced a lynch mob than this kind of thing. You know the kind of things that go on there, perversion and all that. So I didn't want to go and the authorities *knew* why we were in jail—we were not criminals—and *knew* that we shouldn't be put in that kind of situation, and that that kind of experience would really be *too much*. Well, we were detained a long time but they eventually decided to send us there. And to me it was just like a nightmare. Some of the things that I saw there I had never seen in my life. I could not even have imagined them. My imagination could not have stretched to that point! That people could be reduced to such a condition.

I spent a couple of nights there but it was like a lifetime. So after that I made my decision to come here. It had been pending until then. I decided I couldn't take it any longer, and if you can't take it you aren't of any use to yourself or anybody else. I felt that if I could get rid of this kind of feeling of rejection inside me then maybe I could do something, whereas living in America I couldn't—not even for myself. You've been here in Ghana long enough to know that you have people of all nationalities here—Ghana's boats are the same way, and on the way over here I saw all those people of different nationalities working together, and it was interesting—I looked on and though I still had this hurt and hostility in me, it sort of simmered down again . . . but it's still there. It's just dormant.

Q: *Well, let me ask you this. I know what is frequently the American reaction to an interracial couple. I've seen a number of interracial couples here—usually Ghanaian-British, and I wonder what the feeling is here about American Negroes and white persons who are married, couples such as your husband and yourself?*

To a Ghanaian, we are both foreigners and they do not concern themselves with such things. Also, we are both called the same thing in their language.

Q: *What's that?*

Abruni. It means "stranger," "white." It doesn't mean *exactly* white, it means more "not from the family." Nothing offensive in itself. They have no word for me. Although I'm dark, *they* think I'm light. When my students talk about it and when I go out in the villages, the people consider me as light . . . white.

Q: *You said that this came to you as a big shock, that you had never considered—you never thought about being regarded here as a "stranger."*

You mean *Abruni.* They'll call you that. If you go into the village you hear it. Still, one of the first things my students said to me was that I'm *beautiful.*

I talk "blackism" a lot. I teach that and I want my students to get to know about black people from different parts of the world. It has always come out in my teachings, as that's one of my main interests. So one of the first things my students said when they had to write papers was that they wanted to go to America. That surprised me. I just couldn't understand *why* they wanted to go to *America*. I suppose because I was so wrapped up in my own feelings. But then I decided that the grass might just seem greener on the other side.

Q: *Is your family still in Florida?*

Yes. My mother is always very active in voter registration. She's been a Democratic committee woman from the time I was in grade school. So I come from a very active family. My father taught me civics in high school—he taught there. I remember the time he taught us the right to petition and my sister and I got up a petition to get rid of the principal. It embarrassed my father but he had taught us that we had a right to petition, so we did!

Q: *What do you miss most about America, here, if anything?*

Nothing but the food. I brought everything you can think of. Practically. I came to *live* in Ghana. When I left America I came to *live,* so I brought everything, everything I own except two pieces of furniture.

I've learned about Africa now. It's been quite an experience. I am a much more mature person now than I was when I first came. It takes experience, and I had always fought the idea that you can't know something without first experiencing it. I influenced so many people to come to Africa before I left the U.S. And now I'm reluctant to have them come. Because it's a shock, coming out of a dream. You have a beautiful dream, you don't ever want to see the inside of it. Well, we do, but if you're wise, you don't really try to go into it.

Q: *You don't encourage them to come now?*

Well, you have to be—I don't know—it takes time. I have so much anxiety about my mother who's visiting me here now because I want her to have just the right feeling about everything here and certainly not the wrong reaction . . . and I sometimes think I'm overdoing it.

You know, you have to fight against the propaganda that you're given about Africa, especially if you come from the South. Now, of course, some of it is true, but there are so many other things about it that are not true. And if you get half-truths, then you can get all kinds of wrong feelings. So I'm anxious for her to see for herself.

Q: *Did you ever make any moves to have your citizenship changed?*

No, but I have two citizenships. I'm Dutch and I'm American. No, I hadn't thought about it. I'm told I automatically became a Dutch citizen when I married a Dutch national and I'm allowed to keep my U.S. passport, too.

I've had several people here ask me whether I was going to take out Ghanaian citizenship, but it was just that people are curious, that's all. You know, it's a very good thing that I live here because I can understand very well now the segregation problem in America. I can understand it so perfectly now.

Q: *Really?*

Yes, because being in Ghana, although, as I said, I was really racked up on the Ghanaian culture, I really don't fit. I just cannot fit. *My* conduct is all different from theirs and they can't cope with me because of my background. And I remember that sometimes when I first came out, I was very hostile, and felt that the Europeans were clinging together and not really mixing with Ghanaians. *I was* mixing but when the glamour wore off I realized that I was very lonely and I had nothing in common with many Ghanaians. You know, like being able to crack a joke and have someone here *really* understand it.

Q: *But I'm trying to get from that point to your state- ment that you understand segregation; how does that help?*

Well, because you go with people you understand. For instance, when my husband would say to me when I first came that if one were an American one would always remain an American, no matter how "anti" he was. I can really mix and enjoy myself better with the Europeans than the Ghanaians, even among the sophisticated ones, because sophistication wears off eventually and you get to a point where the surface of everything is gone and you really get down to what's going on and it's—nothing. Because there are differences between the European cul- ture and that of the white American, too, who lives here— you find you can cling together with them and you have something really in common. They find it out too.

Q: *Many of the experiences you had with white Ameri- cans in the States were negative and I thought that per- haps, because of that conditioning, some of this would be injected into some of your relationships with white Ameri- cans here. Has that been the case?*

The only reason I started talking with white Americans here was because they were the only people here who understood my need. Nobody else could understand what was wrong with me, not physically, mentally. Because of our backgrounds they understood *exactly* how I felt, but nobody else.

Q: *All of them do?*

Well, I was lucky to meet the ones who did. They wanted to be friendly but at first I wasn't interested. I still had my reservations even after we got to be friendly. But I found that we had a lot of things in common. Even so, I have more things in common with Gwen, another American Negro girl who came over as I did.

Q: *You mentioned the food thing.*

Yes. I'm a Southern girl and I like Southern cooking.

Q: *Is there no place here where you can get "soul food"?*

Well, I have a little garden at my house where I have collard greens. Actually, when I was living in New York I used to have collard greens very seldom, but here you see so much land and it's so conducive to growing these kinds of food. One girl had brought black-eyed peas from Monrovia, Liberia, and I got her to give me some of her seeds. These are things you don't eat all the time but sometimes you really crave them, because you don't see them often.

That kind of food is definitely a part of our Negro culture and I think it's so beautiful. But often we Negroes do not ourselves realize the value of it. It's sort of like many people who live in New York but do not really appreciate the culture there. Here, you appreciate—not American culture particularly, but the *Negro* culture, and this is something that's missing among us at home. We have a tendency not to appreciate our own culture. We feel embarrassed, and shy. I've heard Ghanaians talking in New York and they would say, "Listen, you come to my place and have plaintains and foo foo and groundnuts" . . . even though they were in America and could get anything, they wanted *their* food! I am here and I demand that they respect my wanting *my* food. Not that I want to eat it every day.

All the Afro-Americans I know here, I've come to know through their visiting me to get soul food. They know I love cooking and they love eating here. So even though I live twenty miles from Accra, the capital, lots of people will come out, just for the food.

Q: *Do you get to hear the kind of music you like here?*

I like rock 'n' roll and I brought lots of records with me. I like Brooke Benton, the Drifters and the Platters, and Ray Charles. I like predominantly black records. Everything black. When I was in New York I had a black apartment because I felt that way. I felt I was surrounded by things white and I needed to balance myself by having black.

Q: *You talk about this tremendous tension that you had there, I wonder if there's anything about not having this tension here, that you miss?*

Oh, no. I never had such peace as I had the first four months I was here. I felt as if I could really, really accomplish something. This was in the first months, when all the glamour was there; after that the smoothness rubbed off and all the roughness came out. Now I'm putting everything together that I've learned here and fitting it together again to work out a philosophy. No, I don't miss anything about the tension. Because I'm a very emotional person and without this tension I can do more.

Q: *But doesn't being a black person in a black society afford you some security?*

No, I'm still "different." In one way I kind of like it but in another way I kind of resent it. Here if I go to the hospital everybody else will be put aside and I will be treated first. Another woman will come up just as sophisticated as I am—if I may say I'm sophisticated—and she will have to wait a long time.

Q: *In other words, they spot you as a foreigner and give you preference?*

It's the way I dress. I don't dress any differently here than I did at home—though very seldom do I wear Ghanaian dress here. I wore it all the time in New York. But here, you see, you lose your identity when you fit into the group. I am not for losing my identity. I don't have very much but I don't want to lose what little I have. If I put on a Ghanaian dress, I am taken for something else—a Ghanaian—and not accepted as I am. In America, I used to be conspicuous also but in a sort of positive way. Still, sometimes I wear a Ghanaian dress for a change.

Q: *What is their reaction when you do?*

They love the idea of my putting on their dress.

Q: *Did you ever meet any of the people in the Peace Corps?*

I don't like the Peace Corps. I've had my quarrels with them. You know the Peace Corps originated during the crisis of the racial demonstrations in America, and it just seemed such bad taste to send people abroad for good will when it was so needed at home. So I was one of those people who were against it. I felt they should spend as much money on good will in our own country. Then, too, there aren't that many Negroes abroad in the Peace Corps either. Even here. There are about two in the whole country. The rest of them are white. And it's *our* people who need to come and see what Africa is like. Well, the others need to, too, but we're the ones who need to learn about our African ties. I guess I have my quarrels with everything.

Q: *You want the Negro American to come into the Peace Corps?*

Yes. Because Ghanaians are suspicious. I'm always asked, "Were you hired by the American government?" And when I say "No, the Ghanaian government," there's always a different response. They always ask me this. Because there is something to respect about a person if you come on your own—there is a big difference.

I came to Ghana with twenty dollars. I was determined to come. I figure if you have something to offer, you are going to manage. I was never one to say if you wanted to do something, don't do it, just because you didn't have all the means.

My new job that I've been accepted for is as a research assistant at the university and also to lecture on a couple of courses on child development and child psychology. My skills are really in early childhood education, but of course child development and child psychology come into this. They are planning this in the curriculum for next year, and they want people who are really interested in this. They are smart enough to realize now that this is really an important thing. Early childhood education involves teaching the child from ages two to five. This is where you build all your concepts. They have nursery schools here but they're like the nursery schools that were in the United States during the war, where the children just play and that's it. Nothing creative goes on.

Q: *Can they afford to do the sort of thing you'd like to do?*

Well, they can do it if I can get people interested in it. The government can afford it, of course—if they can spend money on a lot of other things, they can spend money on this. Education is the most important thing. They can *afford* it, but they probably won't. It's a long-term investment and they want results right away.

Q: *Do you intend to live in Ghana permanently?*

I think we'll go back to America eventually and I'll really do what I wanted to do. I'm in a much better position to do it now. With this kind of experience behind me, I feel that I will be more successful now. Before, I think I would have been torn between two or three different things and my main concern is with education, not civil rights. That's something that I shouldn't have to worry about.

Dr. Robert E. Lee:

GHANA

*Dr. Robert E. Lee, forty-six, and his wife live in a
comfortable residential section of Accra, Ghana, to which
the Lees came in 1955, four years after the country—then
the British colony called the Gold Coast—became self-
governing and two years before it achieved actual independence. Dr. Lee and his wife are both dental surgeons
and their practice includes many of the foreigners resident
in Accra.*

*A man of slight build who seems to radiate a quiet
intensity, Dr. Lee speaks in soft but firm cadence of his
experiences in America and Africa. Sometimes he has to
stop and search for a word, as if years of speaking one of
the local languages has made him unsure of his own.
Speaking a local Ghanaian language is but one of Dr. Lee's
ways of trying to break through the subtle barriers that
can sometimes bar the newcomer's penetration of intimate
African life. Wearing the toga-like Ghanaian robes is*

another. In addition, he has become a Ghanaian citizen.

In Accra, the Lees are popular with Ghanaians and black Americans alike and prominent Ghanaians drop into his home to banter and exchange views with the robed ex-American whose admiration for their country and its people is so evident.

The black American expatriates in Ghana look upon Dr. Lee as the dean of them all by virtue of his long residence there and his close ties with Ghanaians. "He's been helpful in keeping some of us out of trouble," one of them told me. "We go to him when we have problems and he keeps us straight. A lot of the things you might do at home you don't do here, and Dr. Lee tells us the Ghanaian way to go about it."

Dr. Robert E. Lee

Q: *Were you active in the civil rights movement in America?*

I was not technically affiliated with groups who made that their objective. But, you know, during your schooldays you support those who are talking about the things that affect you. You support the NAACP and various groups who are doing the things you think need to be done, who seem to be interested in the uplift of your people.

Q: *You were a dental surgeon in New York City?*

I practiced in Brooklyn for about fourteen years before I came here. I had gone to Lincoln University in Pennsylvania and Meharry College in Nashville, Tennessee.

Q: *Lincoln seems to have turned out quite a number of civic leaders in its time.*

Lincoln University is one of the best schools Negroes have in America. It's not the biggest but it's one of the few schools that I know of that lets you grow up to be a *man*. It influences you to feel that it is necessary for you to speak out, to belong to a society and to make your little influence in it felt. When you come out, it's with the feeling, "Well, I finished Lincoln, therefore I must go out and do something." You can't just say, "Well, I finished Lincoln," and that's that. When I left Lincoln in 1942 I was twenty-two. After that I went to Meharry during the war years. Then in forty-five I did my internship in New York and started practicing about 1947.

You know, very few Afro-Americans have many real contacts with Africans. What most of them know is what they've picked up at the movies. There is not much awareness concerning Africans and Africa. It was a shock to me, coming from South Carolina as I did, when I met Africans as students at Lincoln. It was an inspiration to me to meet them. I had been told all the things that all of us have been told about Africans and was surprised to find it wasn't so. They had some of the same disadvantages I had and a few more advantages. I began to look at this thing a bit more realistically. So I got to know them and I spoke to them quite a bit about how things were in their home, Africa. Many are famous now—Kwame Nkrumah was there—others are names that you probably know. One is now minister of aviation in Nigeria; another is a commissioner of railroads in Nigeria. One is with the Development Corporation here; another is a professor at the University of Ghana. Oh, quite a few of them are around. I knew and talked with them when they were there at Lincoln University.

Q: *Were you thinking about emigrating even at that time?*

No. I was thinking mostly about how I was going to stay out of South Carolina! And how I could be independent so that I could work for *me* and I wouldn't have to get a job, because in my town you worked for some white fellow, and from my experience that relationship was never very friendly or very nice.

Q: *Was your particular experience in South Carolina rougher than most?*

I would say that my experience in South Carolina was mostly from my observation, you see. Negroes soon learn how to build their own private little wall around their sensitive little places so that you can't injure them, even though you are standing right next to them. But you can see through the wall, it's nothing. But because I could see it doesn't mean that I actually experienced it myself. I left as a young boy and I grew up in a family that looked after me. You learn how to avoid things like street fights and all. In a little town like mine, everybody knows everybody and the town, Charleston, is not altogether segregated like many towns. The people live all mixed up and even though you're separate, you're not segregated, completely, like say in Harlem.

So one might have neighbors who were white. They're there, but they're not there. You're there, but you're not there. So you can observe, in your little day-to-day contacts, and you come to know about the situation. You don't rock the boat; you see what happens to those who do rock the boat. So you just wait until you can get your boat on the ocean. Then you just float it on out of there. Or you stay down there and fight as some of my friends have. They and their children are the ones now who are involved in freedom sit-ins and things like that. I know many of these people, I know their parents. But some of us decided that there are better ways to fight this struggle. Many of us believe, as I believe, that the nucleus, the center, of the struggle is not there. The battle will never be won *there*. It will be the *outside* pressures that will make things get better. I am one of those who believe that.

I went on away and finished medical school and finished dentistry. . . . I got married and went into practice in New York. My wife and I had been classmates at Meharry Medical School. Then in New York I met some other Africans. By then World War Two was over and things were beginning to happen in the world. So I ran into an African here and there, some of the old friends I had while I was a student, people who congregated around New York. You meet diplomats from Liberia. You run into these people. I was interested in these people so we began to cooperate in little groups that worked to establish contacts among black students. We got on committees that helped African students. Then the Korean War came along and I went into the Army. That was the first time that I ever had two years to do what I liked. I was in the Army Medical Corps. I just did dentistry and that was all.

I was stationed down in Georgia, but that wasn't too bad because I knew all the people down there, like the rabbit in the briar patch. So I thought about it then, in the Army. It was quite all right on the post. There were little racial things of the sort you can pick up anywhere in America, but I would say generally people bent over backwards with the officers. But once I got off the base, it was still Georgia, there was no doubt about that. There might have been a little hesitation on the part of, say, the police officers to attack you if you were in uniform. They would give you trouble but they wouldn't just attack you, as I've seen happen to black people in civilian clothes. But normally I was on my way somewhere. I was never just "on the

town" so to speak. I was never just going into Savannah—
the camp was outside Savannah. I was going *somewhere*
every time I left the post, either to someone's house in
Savannah or to my mother's in Charleston, a few miles
away, or to some place where I knew people. I'd first make
sure my car was all right, then I'd take off and wouldn't
stop until I got there. I knew from my youth how to travel
in the South. I wouldn't stop at restaurants and all that
business. I'd just fill my tank and take off. Or if I did have
to stop for petrol, or to go to a toilet, I would make sure it
was in a fair-sized town. I wouldn't stop on the highway.
During that period in the Army I was thinking about
Africa. When I got home I told my wife that if we were
going to do anything about it, we'd better do it now, while
we're young.

I resumed my contact with one or two of my former
classmates, Africans. I met them and we talked about my
going with them and the things that were going on in
Africa, the trouble in the Gold Coast. You could get first-
hand information that was more accurate than the newspapers. You could get it by word of mouth or by writing. I
began to write and my interest heightened. It was then
that I decided that this whole business of race discrimination, racialism and all these inequities, were probably
directly tied to what was going on in Africa. I agreed with
what the Africans were doing about it. I saw that Afro-
Americans couldn't do these things, couldn't solve their
problems in the same way. And so I decided to come here
and pitch in here.

Q: *Why Ghana?*

I came to Ghana because I knew more people here.
These people in Ghana had gotten further along the road
to self-government, and I could come here at *their* invitation. Whereas, if I'd tried Nigeria, I would've had to go

through Britain—or if to French Africa, through France. And they would never have let me stay—not with these thoughts! That's why I came to Ghana. I knew Kwame Nkrumah, I knew several other people I've mentioned already.

Q: *Did they help you to come?*

They didn't help me to come but they encouraged me. They said, "Don't you pack up your things and move to Africa. After all, you've never been to Africa. What you should do is come over and *visit*. Stay as long as you like. *Then* you can decide what you're going to do."

So I did. I came over alone for about three or four months and I saw some of the people I mentioned and they made sure I got around. I went all around; I saw it; I liked it, and I thought that I would be very . . . inspired living here. It was about 1952 or '53. You could *feel*, when you came here, that these people weren't kidding, that they were quite capable. They knew exactly what they were doing. The struggle they were conducting was not thrust upon them; it was calculated that it would work out, as such struggles work out. After that visit I went back to my wife and said, "I think we can be happy here."

So we began to pack up our things. We remained in the U.S. for a couple of more years, but we finally set out and I sent my family on ahead. (I have two boys. The oldest is twenty-one.) My wife and the two children came ahead of me while I stayed home and finished up the house and the office business that I had. Then I came over here.

Q: *What made the biggest impression on you when you first came to Ghana?*

As I look back over it, when the plane stopped at Dakar, I had a really funny feeling because I didn't know . . . really . . . what to expect. Even though I'd spoken to my African friends, I still didn't know what to *really* expect. I mean, I would have known if I were going to Paris, I should expect subways and buses in the streets and French-speaking policemen, night clubs and schools and things like that. People eating in restaurants, the usual things. But here in Africa I didn't know what everyday life would be like—I just had faith that I would find things would be okay, because all my friends were okay. And if they are okay, I'm okay.

In the Dakar airport I noticed that Africans were the ones loading the planes; in New York I didn't see that. I noticed they were also the ones servicing the aircraft that came into the airport. And you saw them behind a desk now and then. You don't see that when you come into *New York*. At least you didn't in those days. Now I understand it's changed quite a bit.

Q: *How would you describe the kinds of black expatriates who come to Africa?*

I think there are several types of Afro-Americans who come here. There are those who think that when they get here they are going to find a very primitive situation and that they will be head and shoulders above all the local people. They think that even if they don't have any particular talent in their own environment, they expect in this environment to be better than, more useful than, cleverer than the Africans.

These people are making a great mistake. They become frustrated because they come and find that it is not like that; that we have some clever people here, too, that we have people here just like they are—who think they are clever! Usually these kind of expatriates have a very difficult time because they can't adapt mentally to finding things here as they really are.

Then there are those people who come thinking that they are going to get rich. They've heard all these stories about gold and diamonds in Africa and they picture in their minds, I imagine, that these resources are lying on top of the ground and that the poor old African is walking on them and doesn't know what they are. But that they, coming from the U.S.A., will know what they are, will just pick them up, put them in a bag, and go on back home! When he comes and finds things are not like that, he becomes frustrated also. He sees that there are no more resources sitting on top of the ground here than there are in *his* town and that the people who control these resources are no more gullible than those who control the resources in *his* town.

Then of course there is another type, and I put myself in that group, who come because they feel that there is a positive contribution they might be able to make. This type feels that to help alleviate his own condition he has to help alleviate this one first. Once this one is straightened out and is going in the proper direction, the American one will automatically fall in line, because they're one and the same situation, caused by the same circumstances. The same politics, the same economics govern his situation as govern the situation here. And the same struggle that he is having, even though he thinks his is racial and only that, is going on here.

I don't say that all Afro-Americans think that their situation is only racial, but I do say that the average one walking around the streets thinks that if he was just a white man, he wouldn't have any trouble. I come to that conclusion because he makes so many efforts to be a white man. He pretends that he's not an African at all; if you call him an African, he'll want to fight you about it. He doesn't mind being called a "Negro," but he doesn't want to be called an "African." He spends a lot of time and money trying to change his image. This leads me to believe that he thinks his situation is *racial*.

I understand *why* he thinks that. But I think that that's

not really the crux of the matter. The real crux of the matter is political and economic. And the same politics and economics control the African as control the black man in the U.S.A. or in England or wherever he finds himself. And when the African, in Africa, changes the image, it automatically changes the black man's image over there. Some of us see it that way and feel that we will spend the rest of our lives trying to contribute to the alleviation of that situation *in Africa.*

Q: *Then you don't feel the race problem in America will be solved in America, but abroad?*

I don't think that, left alone, the Afro-American will solve the race problem in America. It isn't within his power to solve it. He doesn't control the areas that control that problem. And he isn't going to control the area that makes that problem necessary. He is a "Negro," and he is going to be a "Negro," for he *must* be a "Negro" for the thing to operate. He cannot change and be something else, for then the whole thing changes, you see. Because the fact that the thing operates the way it does makes him the "Negro," and is why he cannot escape that. He'll be the "great Negro scientist," the "great Negro singer," the "great Negro fighter," the "great Negro baseball player," but he'll always be a "Negro." Everything will have this stamp on it to remind him of the fact, and even those who speak obviously in his interests, in a friendly manner, will talk about "our Negroes."

Q: *Why must he be a Negro "for the system to operate," as you say?*

Why? Because that's the whole reason for the system. I'll go back to the preslave era before Western or European slavery, and I'm including U.S. slavery in that. People didn't pay much attention to those things. Look at the old maps. Years ago, centuries ago, they referred to the "Ethiopes." Now this was Abyssinia. The whole continent was called Ethiopia or Abyssinia or Guinea or some such name. But you don't see any reference to "Negro." This "Negro" business started after the slavery run. The Africans who found themselves in the U.S.A. belonged to a particular type of slavery. You can show that it was slightly different from the very same Africans held in slavery in, say, South America or in other places.

Q: *What about the way slavery was practiced in Africa?*

At that time they were not held in slavery here in Africa. The word "slave" has had a different meaning at different times. Slavery was then an industry in the U.S.A., not a condition of oppression, but an industry. Whereas the type of slavery that existed here in Africa, as I understand it, existed among people involved in little petty wars who were taken prisoner, *those* people were called slaves. The word in the Ashanti language for "war prisoner" is the same as that for "slave." They were taken as their penalty for losing the war. But the Africans in the U.S. did not lose a war with the Americans. They were not at war with the Americans or the English.

Let's say you had a fight between two different language groups or tribal groups and one side won. You took from that place so many captives, so many prisoners of war. Usually they took over the village, much like the Europeans used to do when they were conquering a territory. They took over the whole area and the people in the area became their subjects. Those who were in the most honored position used the labor of these people. But as time went on, the slaves blended in with that population and became part of that civilization.

So he was not a slave because of color. He could be a white man but he wouldn't be a slave because he was a white man. He was a slave because he found himself in a certain situation and he lost. He could be a slave because he owed somebody some money and until he worked out that debt he would be in that man's service. But even then there were rules that applied. The Spanish slave system, the Portuguese system followed rules. The slave owners didn't make the rules. The church or society made the rules.

But the Afro-American slave situation was a different thing; it was a perpetual, forever degrading system and even today you can see it, it's still there. And it will be there as long as the economic arrangement remains as it is. It remains like in an apartheid South Africa. The Negro is in a Bantustan, he's in a "Negro-stan." You have Harlems all over the place and they are that way for a reason. It isn't that all Negroes decide they like Negroes and they're going to all move to Harlem; people don't do that. That is not human nature. Because the Negro in America is a man who can speak English; he eats breakfast, eggs and bacon, like white people; he goes to the theater; he goes to baseball games; he drinks beer and looks at television. He does the same things everybody else does. So there's no need for him to go around with Negroes just because he's a Negro. Or because he's the only one that speaks "Negro."

Everybody likes jazz, including white people, so it isn't that only Negroes play jazz and so they want to go around with Negroes because "they play the music I like." He's in Harlem for an economic reason and he's purposely in Harlem. He's purposely in Chicago on the South Side, he's purposely in Los Angeles where he is. He went to Los Angeles for his own reasons but he wound up in Watts for another reason beyond his control. This is why the housing fight is so big; the housing fight is a serious fight; you break that one and you've gone a long way toward breaking this "Negro-stan," these highly segregated, highly concentrated Negro areas where Negro labor is the same as it was during the slave trade, they just don't call it slavery. But the bulk of Negroes cannot control their work. That's why many of us go into medicine and teaching, and preaching. We feel independent. We don't want to get into that thing. We want to try to be as free as we can within the circumstances.

I think that my children, growing up here, are actually growing up in a freer mental environment. Freer from this standpoint: Nobody grows up in a totally free society, that is, to do what he likes, think as he likes, there's no place like that. We all know that. But here in Africa a black child grows up in an environment that is not set up to make him hate himself. He is free from that. He doesn't have to form any special image of himself because in this society, where we live now, there isn't even any antiwhite feeling. The people here aren't even mad at white people. They don't have racialism, they don't seek out people on the basis of color here at all. They pick you out on the basis of your cultural background. They know you are different because you don't speak a local language, you don't have their eating habits, their sleeping habits, their other cultural habits, so they know you're not one of them. But that doesn't mean they are mad at you. They're not going to go out of their way to do you in because you don't belong to their tribe. While they're not going to let you marry their daughters, if possible, they aren't going to lynch you if their daughter likes you. They're not going to penalize her either and if you have any children, they're not going to put the children on the streets. That's the way it is.

My children, therefore, can grow up freer in their outlook on the world. Right now they can accept any friends in their community. And there are all kinds of people here, people from everywhere in the world living in this town. They have contact with them in school and in their social activities. They can choose whom they like, and people can choose them if they like them. If they don't like them, they just don't come around.

Q: *Are black Americans still regarded as American?*

I think it depends on the person. You can probably cite many examples of people who have lived here for years and have never been accepted into the inner circles of African society. But part of that is their own fault. There are certain prerequisites to being an African. Some of them I just mentioned. If you want to really belong to the society you can do it. But if you don't speak their language and if you don't agree with whatever their customs are, there is no point in your being around. Why should they want you? Maybe you are a nice guy to meet at a cocktail party and all that, but there's no place for you in the family. They'd have to speak English when you are around and after a while that becomes tiring. It's like they're carrying you on their backs, you see. But you can make it easy for yourself and for them by learning the language. Just the few words I've learned in the local language immediately opened up many doors. Because if you can speak a local language they don't see you as an American any more. The minute you can speak their language, even if you speak with an accent, all of the formal etiquette, all of the reserve goes. And you see the person as he really is.

Q: *Is there any animosity directed toward you when relations between Ghana and the U.S. go bad?*

Not to me, personally. But many Afro-Americans, though they are mad at the U.S.A., still defend it. America doesn't know how lucky it is to have Afro-Americans. They are the most loyal people—I don't understand them. I don't see how it is that they allow themselves to be

beaten for so many years and still be loyal. Even if my
mother did that to me, I would leave her. But Afro-
Americans are not like that, that is, the average one. He
can be annoyed at what has happened to someone in the
U.S.A. or at some situation involving the U.S.A. in international affairs but if people attack the U.S., they must
only attack it on the thing *he* attacks it on.

Q: *But isn't that true of people generally, of Ghanaians
as well?*

Let's make an analogy. Let's take a Ghanaian who has
gotten mad at Ghana and who has left Ghana. If you begin
to attack Ghana, will he defend it? I don't think so, because I read about those who have gone away and who are
mad about one thing or another. They make it a point to
attack everything about Ghana, even the good things, they
will turn them around and make them sound bad. Or they
will say what they think their host country likes, like talking about communist influences in Ghana. They know
there is no such thing; they know it because they have just
left here and they know the people here. But they know
that in certain areas that goes over good.

Most of these people cannot earn a living elsewhere because they have no real skills that could be useful, say, in
New York City. So you must *give* them a job, you must
give them a position in your industrial society for him to
even eat. So he maneuvers, but the Afro-American
won't do that here, even if he wants a job. If you attack the
U.S.A. you better attack it on the *racial* problems. Because
if you attack it on another thing, such as the reason for
World War Two, or the problems in Vietnam, or its image
of China—the Afro-American will have the same image the
U.S.A. has of China, he'll hand you the same story about
the "starving Chinese." Because he's like that.

Q: *You have talked about some of the strengths of life*

here. Have you found any negative things in Ghanaian society?

Well, I think that some aspects of the old African society do not work well in a new industrial situation, the emphasis on clan and tribe, for example. Tribalism can be used by Africa's enemies to divide her people.

The Afro-American is a good example of this. In America they're not Yorubas or Ibos any more, they're now all *Negroes.* They have no strength, except as Negroes, which they're trying to build now. They're trying to make themselves into a unit. But even now a lot of *their* intellectuals are talking against it; they don't want them to be Negroes. The Malcolm X faction wants them to be *Negroes;* the Marcus Garvey faction wants them to first be *Negroes.* On the other hand, what was in the old days the W. E. B. Du Bois faction, now the Martin Luther King faction, and the Roy Wilkins faction—they don't want them to be Negroes, they want them to be "just plain Americans!" This is not a realistic approach to the problem, because they are not that. Even if *they* think they are, the rest of the American people don't think they are.

Q: *Have you found the things you sought, by and large, when you came to Ghana?*

I have not found everything, not by a long shot, that I sought when I came to Ghana. But I *do* see the superstructure that holds a promise for the future. There are many criticisms, there are many holes which I think if corrected would make the operation run more smoothly and simply. But when I came here I wasn't a child, I was a grown man, and I had been working with people for years. I didn't come here expecting to find all the Africans perfect. Nor did I expect them to have all the answers to all their problems, even some of the problems that bothered me. But I did see that they understood what the root of this trouble is. And I see that some effort is being made. Even at a great sacrifice.

Ghana is going through some difficult readjustments, but the people here don't seem afraid to go through them. They don't seem afraid of making the sacrifice; they don't seem afraid to withstand the onslaught of those who may wish that Ghana does not succeed. They don't seem to be afraid to speak out and to attempt to convince their own people that they have value, that they have worth, that they can accomplish certain things. And this is what they're doing.

What I wanted to get out of it, I'm getting out of it. I'm sure you're aware that as a dental surgeon I wouldn't have left New York to come to Accra if I wanted money. Anybody knows that if you just want to make money you can make more in New York City than in Accra.

Q: *Do you feel that you get enough stimulus, enough opportunities to exchange information with others in your profession?*

I have to say no, I don't, because the dental community is very small and there are only two private dentists in the whole country. The others—about thirty, spread all around the country—are all in the government service. So there isn't much communication in the profession; my contacts are in the whole field of medicine, with physicians and people like that, because I don't look at dentistry any more as a separate individual profession. It has become only a part of an over-all public health team approach which involves dentists, doctors, workers, nurses and so forth. I'm falling behind in the newer things in modern dentistry as it's practiced in my former country because I don't have many contacts. Whenever I get a chance to visit, though, I go around and check on most of the new gadgets and whatever new techniques there are. When I can, I pick up whatever new texts I can get my hands on.

Q: *Do you feel the African revolution has had a direct effect on the Afro-American's revolution?*

Oh, yes, except that I don't think the Afro-Americans have what you would call a "revolution" except in a social sense, in the change from the original relationships between them and the Europeans in America. And in the new relationships still being worked out. But not in the true *revolutionary* sense, that is, of there being some great change in the over-all socio-economic structure. What they had in Cuba was a revolution, the Chinese have a revolution, the Africans had a revolution—they are actually changing an entire socio-economic situation. Their success is having a profound effect on the Afro-American and his fight to get equal and fair, decent treatment.

Because now you cannot lynch an Afro-American with impunity. Now the world knows about it. On the radio and TV here you always hear talk about Afro-Americans. If you beat up an Afro-American, we are going to know about it. Somebody here is going to talk about it . . . in the U.N. or someplace. That's what I mean. And I think that Afro-Americans ought to appreciate this—that's one of the most important aspects of their struggle. And they should rather turn their attention and cooperate regardless of what the majority of Americans think or say about it. They should not fall for all these stories about whether Africa is going to go communist or not. That does not concern the Afro-American. At this stage in his development I don't think he's involved. That's the Cold War business. Ours, the Afro-American's, is first, relief from oppression, and it's directly related to the African struggle. I'm talking specifically about Afro-American problems. When the

Russians and those people have a revolution, the Afro-American doesn't pay any attention, that's a different class of people. When the Chinese were having theirs, it didn't mean much to the Afro-American. But when the Africans started—ah! it's a different thing. He subconsciously feels that identity, even though it isn't popular for him to express it all the time. Inside, he knows it. And their leadership should constantly call it to their attention. Some have tried. Malcolm X was one and I considered him a leader. He hit the nail on the head about this thing.

Afro-Americans who try to play down that identity are missing the point. I don't think anybody is encouraging Afro-Americans to all get on a ship and come to some parts of Africa. I don't think there is any sensible leader in Africa or anywhere who would make that proposition as a solution. Neither do I think it is clever for the Afro-American to think this. But I think it is incumbent upon him to note that "whither we go, he goes." If we Africans go up, he goes up. If we go down, he goes down. No matter what the Chinese do, or the Russians do, or the English do, I think that what Africans do are the things that have direct effect on the Afro-American.

Bill Sutherland:

TANZANIA

In 1958 I was an observer at the first All-African Peoples' Conference, convened in Accra, Ghana, where a cross section of the continent's political, labor and tribal leaders gathered to talk about their mutual concerns. It was a significant gathering. For many of the young African politicos, this was their first trip outside their own countries (though an independence movement was building, most African states were still under colonial rule). It was the first time such a large number of nationalist leaders from the English- and French-speaking African territories had met together; indeed, it was a time of introduction for many young activists who spoke the same political language but came from opposite sides of the vast continent.

On the staff of the secretariat provided for the conference by the Ghana government was a young, bespectacled American Negro who hustled around the meeting halls helping to ease the myriad snags that inevitably occur in any undertaking so large and diverse. His name was Bill Sutherland.

Sutherland was then personal secretary to Ghana's minister of finance and was married to one of the country's young cultural leaders. (The Sutherlands have since separated.) Bill Sutherland, a pacifist, has firm liberal views and acts upon them, sometimes at great personal cost. He served three years in a Federal prison for his opposition to service in World War Two, part of which time was spent in solitary confinement because of his challenges to racial segregation within the prison itself.

After his years in Ghana, Sutherland took up residence in Tanzania, where he is now an official of that East Africa nation's information ministry. Although there are a few American Negroes working for other African governments, he is perhaps unique among them in having worked in two such governments, first in West Africa and now in East Africa. His reflections are born of an intimate involvement with life on that continent, in all its fulfillment and frustrations.

Bill Sutherland

Q: *Do you really feel you will continue to be a resident in Africa?*

I don't think I will ever be part of the American scene again.

It took me a very long time to arrive at that decision. From about 1940 to 1953 I was involved in various civil rights movements, for thirteen years, and I felt the object was to become a first-class citizen in American society, but . . . if I go back a very long way . . . this whole question of being part of an affluent society changed my outlook. I'd had an opportunity to see its results. Like many other Negro families, my family thought that if I was in a better neighborhood, went to the better schools and had that sort of background, I would stand a better chance in the world. So we went to live in an all-white community, a community where all these things were present. But being in that kind of community only increases one's sense of being an alien. People say to me now, "Don't you think about your roots?" Well, I don't think I ever had roots in the sense people talk about; that is, in terms of a community, because the community was always, in a certain sense, alien. There were a few individuals and a few groups such as church groups that accepted me, but I don't think I ever felt, during my life in the United States, part of a larger community.

I went to Bates, where they had a quota system. They were nice and "liberal" there, but, although *I* got in, I was aware of the quota system. I started off my activities on the racial questions by becoming a member of the NAACP, that kind of thing. But the people within the white community, who really seemed to be the people who were genuine, were people who had what at that time might be called a Christian Socialist pacifist point of view, so it was natural for me to gravitate toward them. They went beyond purely racial concerns and I, in turn, because of them, became interested in many other ideas they had, because they touched this sphere where I was most involved.

My family was relatively well off. We had our ups and downs like anyone else, but we were in a community where I had a chance to see what the affluent society really meant *to white people:* how unhappy they were, what ego satisfactions they had and so forth. I had thought about all this since high school.

I got to the point where I rejected the basic values of that society—a society where there were no real connections and friendship; where there was such anonymity, instead of people feeling that they counted for something; where there was so much concern about appearances and so little concern about substance. For me to continually go to jail, get my head beaten in in order to be a part of this, I just felt that it simply wasn't worth it. I had been thinking about Africa ever since I came back from my first trip abroad in 1951, when I met certain African leaders. Before that I didn't know much about it. I had been one of the founding members of New York CORE and had spent three years in prison as a war objector during World War Two. One year had been spent in punishment quarters because I was on strike against racial segregation in the Federal prisons. I was with A. Philip Randolph and Bayard Rustin when we campaigned against segregation in the Armed Forces in 1948. We also campaigned for FEPC laws and to save people from being extradited back to Southern chain gangs. I pursued all of these things and I felt that they were worthwhile because there was hope for the society. But gradually I began to get the feeling that the American way of life wasn't really worth the struggle. And that if there were other places—naturally being an Afro-American and emotionally attached to Africa I thought of that continent—I would go to a place where there was more fluidity, where there was more chance to have the kind of society that *I* believed in. So, as I have tried to explain to some other people, not always successfully, it wasn't simply a *racial* thing that made me leave. Sure, there is a stream of Americans—the William Lloyd Garrisons, the Thoreaus —who were people in that society *I* could identify with, as

I did with the Quakers. But these were the people who were usually in jail most of their lives. They were not the dominant stream in American society and I did not foresee their becoming dominant. These people were the "Africans" in American character. They were people whom you might study, but they do not determine the stream or the direction in which the country is going.

In Fifty-one I was in France and met some of the African leaders in Paris. This was at the time of the Korean War and some of us in America were opposing this war—we were opposing it on the streetcorners—in New York and other places, and we would get a lot of heckling like, "Why don't you go and tell this to the Russians?" "You figure that here you're pretty safe, but if you go tell this to the Russians, you know what will happen to you."

The group that I belonged to had a very presumptuous name, the Peace Mission, and included the late A. J. Muste and others. We thought that this criticism held a valid point. So four of us who had been in prison for opposing the Second World War were selected and we were sent to Europe to present a call to the people on the other side of the Iron Curtain to end the war.

We didn't have it all worked out but we were going to try it. Actually, the gimmick that got a lot of publicity in France at that time was that we were going to bicycle from Paris to Moscow. We cycled from Paris to the German border and there we were stopped by the Allied High Command who didn't want our point of view presented in West Germany. Then we put our bicycles on trains and went around through Switzerland, to Austria.

This was taking a great deal of time and money and we were again stopped in Vienna. The only way we felt we could even give an indication of our position was to ignore these restrictions and boundaries. So we went to Baden, which was the headquarters of the Russians. We had leaflets, printed in Russian, calling on the Russian people to refuse to support the war, and we passed these leaflets around the Russian Army headquarters for about two or three hours without anybody stopping us.

Having gone to Paris and talked to some of the African leaders, I went to England and met more of them. So I would say that my interest in Africa stemmed from this visit to Europe.

Q: *How did you get to Africa?*

Well, I went back to the States in May of 1951, and worked with an organization helping South African resistance people for about a year and a half. After that Bayard Rustin had had an offer to go to Nigeria and work with Nnamdi Azikewe,* and he couldn't make it at the time. I was invited in his place. I went to London in 1953 and met Azikewe in the summer, so that I was present there at the first Nigerian Conference for Independence in August, 1953, and I worked with some of the Nigerian leaders. In spite of the fact that Nigeria had invited me, they were not successful in getting a visa for me from the British, who were still in control. I waited for months, then I finally gave it up and concentrated on Ghana, a country that was a little more politically advanced. Through the intercession of friends I got a visa for Ghana and I went there at the end of 1953.

At that time I didn't really know anything about the Ghanaian revolution. I just thought it would be better to be in Ghana than cooling my heels in London waiting for the Nigerian visa to come through.

I spent six months just being at the University in

---

* Now President of Nigeria

Ghana, trying to see if there was a place where I could fit in. There came an opening up-country where they were trying to start a school with a different type of educational system than the conventional British approach. They wanted to establish a high school which had an emphasis on practical activity: courses in agriculture, public health and public works and other things. So for two years I tried to make a go of this.

At Shito, as the place was called, I met Efua, the Ghanaian girl who was to become my wife. After about four or five months from the time I came to Ghana, we married. She had been educated both in Ghana and at Cambridge. She went to a teachers' training college in Cambridge and took a two-year course.

I was at the school from the beginning of 1954 until the beginning of 1957, and I met almost absolute resistance from the British who were still influential in the country's ministries even though the Gold Coast [Ghana] had "self-government" status. They didn't accept the idea of this school we were trying to start, that was very much like an Antioch College—but at the high school level—with a work-study program.

Then I got a job with the Ghana Finance Minister, Komla A. Gbedemah, as his personal secretary.

Q: *How long were you there in that job?*

Four years. He was Minister of Finance throughout the time I was employed by him. In sixty I left that job.

I was asked to go to India to speak about another project I had been involved in which was called "Resistance Against the French Explosion of Nuclear Devices in the Sahara." And I was in India for about six weeks during the end of sixty, and the beginning of sixty-one.

When I came back to Ghana in 1961 it was very difficult to find new employment. There was a certain undercurrent of sentiment against Gbedemah even during this period, and I don't know whether my difficulties had to do with him or not. You may recall that he fled the country a year later, after breaking with Nkrumah. For a while I couldn't find a niche that was satisfactory to me. Then I got an offer from Israel to go there and help as an adviser to them on the African program being put on by the Histradrut, Israel's equivalent of the AFL-CIO.

It was also at this time that the Non-Violent League, which I was connected with, got the idea of setting up another group known as the World Peace Brigade, to see what the possibilities were of "direct action," much along the lines of what we see so much of in the United States today, but on an international level. One of their first ideas was that we should work along with those people in Africa who were part of the freedom movement out there. Presidents Julius Nyerere of Tanganyika and Kenneth Kaunda of the now Zambia were people who were interested in this approach.

So I left Israel in 1962 and came to Addis Ababa, Ethiopia, to be an observer at a conference of the Pan-African Freedom Movement for East and Central Africa. It was at this conference that I met Kaunda again. I had been in touch with him and he had asked Britain's Reverend Michael Scott, Bayard Rustin and myself to help in a campaign for the freedom of what is now Zambia. Our efforts were coordinated from a base, here in Dar es Salaam, Tanganyika, which I ran. When that struggle was over I remained here in Dar es Salaam to become an employee under contract to the Tanganyika government.

At this point in my life I would like to get back into some nongovernmental role. At the moment I am an assistant secretary in the Ministry of Information and Tourism. In addition, ever since I've been in the government, I have been given special duties. I worked first in the office of the Tanzanian Second Vice-President with alien refugee groups who were trying to settle in this country, among them the Kikuyus of Kenya. I have also been sent to Geneva to help negotiate with the U.N. concerning aid to these refugees and at one point, later on, I was assigned to the Tanganyika delegation to the United Nations.

Q: *Have you reflected much on your Ghanaian experience and what you derived from it?*

First, I discovered that this emotional idea of identification that I had was a little bit out of whack, historically. During the early period of the late W. E. B. Du Bois and Marcus Garvey, there was this idea of a *color-based* Pan-Africanism, a feeling of unity among people of African descent all over the world. I came along when it was changing from a color thing to a continental thing. In 1947 there was a conference in Manchester, England, which Nkrumah attended along with other African leaders, and at that point the *African* leaders took over the Pan-African movement. Prior to that time *West Indians,* such as the late George Padmore, had been dominant on the African nationalist scene. The West Indians were more than willing and happy to see the African leaders coming up and taking over, but it did change the whole Pan-African idea from a *universal* unity of colored people to a *continent*-wide unity. This was one factor which really changed my idea of what *I* could do in Africa, since *I* was not an *African* or from this continent.

Second, I hadn't been aware—though I soon became aware—of another fact: there had been a great deal of African alienation from Afro-Americans in West Africa because of the Liberian situation: the fact that over a long period of history "Americo-Liberians"—ex-American slaves resettled in Liberia—had behaved in the same way colonial rulers had elsewhere. Other Africans knew this and reacted negatively to it. Let me put it this way: the emotional attachment of the man on the street here was still the same. If you were Afro-American and you came over and talked to somebody, there would be a real warmth of expression. But among the more politically aware people, there was a wary look that spelled caution.

There was one other thing that I'm going to have to acknowledge: that in the previous period before I ever came to Ghana, there had been some Afro-Americans who had come to Ghana and who had pulled some fast deals. I'm afraid that those of us who came after these men had to suffer because of the actions which they took. However, I will say this, that as far as the Pan-African activity was concerned, I felt very much a part of it; because the late George Padmore, the West Indian who encouraged African nationalism, had been invited down to Ghana by Nkrumah. He was a very trusted person and I did a great deal of work with him at several Pan-American conferences. The opportunity to meet leaders from all over the continent and to work with them was great and I got a lot of insights in Ghana. And, of course, I did marry a Ghanaian and I was able, through my family relationships, to get a certain feel of the people and of the country.

Q: *You come in from outside the society and you marry a person who's Ghanaian. Family ties mean much in Africa and you would not have these ties, especially the tribal tie. How does this affect you?*

Well, first of all there's a very natural fear of the outsider on the part of the family. They don't know who he is or why he has come. Because my wife, who was a Fanti, was very much a strong personality and because she was very much respected by her family, I think I had a degree of acceptance which might not have been usual. I think it's also true that had I been a member of the Fanti tribe I would have been accepted more easily. But if I had been, say, of the Ga tribe I would have had more problems than I did as a foreigner. I would say that as far as my wife's family is concerned, they really did everything possible to make me feel one of them.

Q: *What are the pros and cons of being an American in a government in Africa? Let's put it this way: you are an educated person, you have held a substantial job in a country which itself had young men possibly wanting the same kind of job. Would not such young men have feelings of jealousy and envy and try to get you ousted, perhaps using the fact that you were a foreign person?*

I think that whatever my problems were about being an American, they would have been the same for any foreigner.

Q: *But Americans do occupy a certain role in the world and have a certain African policy, and I would expect that people react to you differently as an American than if you were of some other nationality.*

When I worked for Gbedemah, it wasn't so much in evidence. As I mentioned before, the problem of people being cautious about Afro-Americans has also expressed itself here in Tanzania. Less, I think, when they got to know me, but there were also certain factors having to do with my own personality, because I wasn't content to just stay in the background. If there were certain things that I thought were wrong, I tended to speak up about them. This did cause a certain amount of trouble, but never enough that I was ever deported.

Q: *Have you any thoughts on the role an expatriate can play, politically, in a newly adopted country?*

When you go into a country where America's foreign policy has definitely rubbed the leaders and the people the wrong way, naturally you would have a very rough, tough row to hoe if you became active politically. But even in West Africa, I can see differences. I can see where a person might be able to take a much more active role in Nigeria than he would, say, in Ghana at this particular time. But I think, first of all, that one would have to remain in the country for a good length of time and have the people get to know you fairly well because, after all, there is this idea of "outsiders." Particularly there is this feeling in parts of Africa that America is going to use its Afro-Americans as a possible "fifth column" or something of that sort, and use them and their color to get "in."

Q: *Has that feeling gotten stronger over the years you've been here in Africa?*

I don't think in general that it's as strong in East Africa as it is in West Africa. I don't mean to imply that if a man comes out to East Africa and he's, let's say, a U.S. Embassy employee or a U.S. Information Service employee that he will have an easy time, because there's no question but that the suspicion is very definite.

Q: *What would be your observation on the ability of the Afro-American to get along with Africans? How would you rate the Afro-American vis-à-vis the white American coming here in an official capacity for the U.S. Government? Does it make a difference if you're white or black and is the difference positive or negative?*

I'm convinced that it does make a difference and that the difference is negative. Let's relate this, to, say, American policy in the Congo, to which most Africans object. Let's say you are an American government employee and you are an Afro-American. It's your job to interpret the American point of view on your government's actions in the Congo. When you do that and you're black, it somehow becomes much worse than if you were a white American.

As a black man who is also a U.S. official, what is one

going to say about the racial situation in the United States? Are you going to point toward the "positive" things at a time when there are riots or there are Selmas? If one is an Afro-American, it's a very tough thing to handle.

When I came here there was an accusation of an American plot here; that America was plotting against Tanzania. At that time they had American officials going around to the houses where Americans were living alerting them. One came to me and handed me a mimeographed paper saying that there was information that there were going to be anti-American riots and demonstrations and that I absolutely shouldn't go downtown. He said that he was the warden of the area and he had come to find out where my house was so I could be evacuated if need be. This was part of the Embassy plan for safeguarding American nationals.

As far as I was concerned, my first reaction to him was simply to tell him that I was sure he had many other people to handle and that he should sort of pass by my house. But I didn't say anything to *him* because he wasn't responsible. I did get to some of the Embassy people I knew and asked them what the hell was going on. They said, "Well, after all, we've had experience with these things in Asia and so we wanted to be sure you were all right." So I said to my American Embassy friends, "*If* you were really concerned about *me,* then what you should do is to set up your machinery in Mississippi and Georgia and Alabama. *That's* where I'm really in danger!"

You know, I have attended meetings and I have gone with no hesitation into the middle of Dar es Salaam at the height of disturbances—anti-American ones. The thing is, I'm in more relative danger *in the United States* than I would be here. Now can you imagine somebody who's Afro-American being assigned to some task like that Embassy man had?

Q: *But I know of a few Afro-American officials who have done very well at African posts.*

Perhaps people with exceptional personalities could overcome this built-in liability, this conflict of interest, but generally I would say that it's very difficult during these times. I know that there are various Negro organizations that press to have more and more Negroes sent here. I would say that this is a mistake. I understand these organizations' point of view; they want to have more and more Negroes in the foreign service, but putting it in terms of *Africa,* I think they are making a mistake.

Q: *You are saying, really, that such an individual has almost got to lie, to put the most favorable face on things?*

I would say that the possibility of divided loyalties would weigh heavily on any individual in this sort of situation. If he *doesn't* have divided loyalties, he's not going to be much use anyhow.

The year before last, on the Fourth of July celebration, an Afro-American group that was here decided to boycott the traditional Fourth of July party given at the U.S. Embassy because they felt there was nothing to celebrate. It was to celebrate "Independence" and *they* weren't independent. There was an Afro-American official here who had to develop a diplomatic "illness" because he was in a fix. He didn't know what to do. He didn't know whether to join the Embassy crowd or stay away with his friends. So he pleaded "sick" but he got called on the carpet by his superiors and he had to explain himself anyway. So I don't feel they should come, that is, *as official people.*

Q: *What about the Afro-American who is not a U.S. Government employee?*

There still will be a problem, but it will be less of a

problem for him as time goes on because he will be able to express himself. Then the way he is regarded by the Africans will depend on his own point of view, his own personality, much more.

We—the private people—are in a better position than the official Negroes, but we're not completely out of possible suspicion. One can always be attacked in a certain way. Even though I came with the World Peace Brigade, a private peace organization, I was constantly being confused with the Peace *Corps* and there were all kinds of rumors about the Peace Corps here, some very unfair rumors. From time to time I was linked to supposed "spying" by the Peace Corps. But I must point out that this kind of thing is a universal problem. If you are in the United States and take an active role in some civil rights organizations, in some communities you are immediately going to be thought of as a Communist. So it is not something that is unique here.

Q: *You said earlier that when you came you had "stars in your eyes" and now you don't. What do you mean?*

I mean I no longer have the idea that Africa, as a newly developing and emerging continent, is going to be able to withstand completely the pressures of the way of life that I was opposed to in the United States. There are great forces that operate on this continent and the people within it are in some cases going to build the same kind of society that I opposed in America. But I am convinced of this: one chooses his own battleground. It's not a question of finding a "perfect" society. What you do is say, "It's one world." I'm sure you will agree that the fight for African freedom is inextricably linked up with the fight for human rights in America. So one chooses a place where one feels the situation is more fluid and where one has a better chance of operating. And I've come to this conclusion: as far as I'm

concerned, I feel that here in Africa there are more opportunities for new experimentation, new values, a society
which more represents what I am seeking than the society
I lived in in the United States.

It's not a matter of absolutes at all. It is very much a
matter of degree and how open the chances are.

Q: *You say that in some cases African societies will
develop some of the same things you opposed in America.
Perhaps you can be more specific about which develop-
ments you found disturbing in African countries.*

I'm not speaking so much of color or race. I'm thinking
of the desire for affluence, of the thirst for power. The real
aim in some of these states is to be exactly the same as the
present great powers— only black instead of white.

Q: *What about the graft, the payoffs, one hears of even
in so-called revolutionary states professing austerity?*

When you take not just the African experience, but that
of the world, you find that the more this kind of corrup-
tion and this power-hunger complex seems evident, the
more developed you will find the society surrounding it.
Since these countries say they are "developing" countries,
one wonders what they are "developing" to! But I think
that, as far as I can judge, in Tanzania there is less of this.
Right down the line, I've found it better on this kind of
thing than practically any part of the world. But that
doesn't say that it does not exist here.

Q: *As a black American, what are the things you miss
away from the black community in America?*

I think you can find important lacks in intangibles
like . . . like a certain kind of sense of humor. Of course,
as an *American* and a big-city boy, I miss being able to go
out at one in the morning and get apple pie and a cold
glass of milk. But I have discovered something important
about myself and that is: I don't miss the kind of comforts

and amenities that I find some of my other Afro-American friends missing. They're really not out of that society because they *reject* that society; they're out of it because they want to be a *full part of it* and they can't be. They miss it so therefore they have a kind of love-hate relationship with America that I don't feel I have. What I miss in America, let's say, are my friends in my community. But I don't have a love-hate relationship because my friends are a minority community within America. I miss them because we had an identity of struggle, but we still have it and they know that I still feel a part of them; I just wish that there were more of that type of person over here.

Q: *Do you feel any twinges of conscience about not being there at this time?*

At different times I do. I never, for example, conceived that there would be a Montgomery bus boycott. When I left in 1952, I never thought it possible that what happened would happen in terms of the civil rights struggle. I certainly feel sometimes the great urge to be back there with the people I knew there who are working in that struggle. But nevertheless, I've also overcome that feeling because those very friends that I'm talking about—I see them when I go to the States or they come here, and I communicate with them by letter—indicate to me that this struggle is still one where the basic aim is to become part of *that* society. As long as that's true, I don't feel that that's my place in the world-wide struggle for human rights. As long as American civil rights groups want to be part of a society that I feel is basically rotten, then I don't—although I have an emotional urge to go there, it's not in any sense overpowering.

Q: *Yet as you have already noted, many of these undesirable traits seem to go along with industrialization. May that not happen here?*

The leadership in Tanzania is very aware of this and emphasizes in its village development programs, in its cooperative program, even in the industries they have developed, a different attitude toward human beings. It's not a question of whether they're wholly successful or not, but there is this *effort* and it's made at a very important place in the nation's power structure. There's an awareness among the leadership here of the pitfalls. They are not willing to just say "industrialization at any price!" I think this is very significant and important. I can't say that it's going to be successful, but my God, the only thing you can do these days is throw your weight onto the side that you believe in, because if you don't, you're going to be taxed anyway to do something you don't believe in.

Q: *Has being in Africa, in an all-black country, changed your own racial attitudes?*

Well, I don't know if this is going to be an answer to this question, but I'll come back again to this whole position of white people here. I haven't gone into this question before but I'd like to mention, in relation to it, the visit of CORE's Jim Farmer to Tanzania. When Farmer came here, although he wasn't representing the American Government at all, American officialdom met him at the airport. They arranged for him to see the ambassador and had dinner with him at other times; they had a special meeting to discuss civil rights with the American community, they had certain of the U.S. officials from Zanzibar come to meet him at a luncheon immediately *after* he had gone to Zanzibar to have a meeting with the Second Vice-President of Tanzania. This completely enraged me because I feel that by surrounding him that way the American Embassy really gave him the kiss of death. Their defense was that if they didn't pay proper attention to a prominent Afro-American citizen coming to Tanzania, they would catch it at home from people who, if they had ignored him or hadn't given him the proper VIP treatment, would have said they were prejudiced.

I made strong representations to them that it was time they got a little education in minority psychology. I told them to imagine themselves as a group of Northern Negroes who came, not into Mississippi, but at least into Tennessee, and that as Northern Negroes they had been aggressive in ways that the Tennessee community didn't like. Then a white liberal from the North comes and visits them. I would say that though the white liberal might not be in total sympathy with them, he still might be able to do them some good, but *never* if they fell all over him and tried to monopolize him. I told them it was definitely time that they began to project a little bit and to benefit from the experience of what it meant to be an unpopular minority. Because I think that in the white community here you see people who are so used to being the dominant group that, even with what one assumes are the best intentions, they just acted in a totally stupid way.

I think the experience in Africa is very good for American white people. I think that at least *some* of them may emotionally go through some of the things that Afro-Americans go through in America such as wondering, "Why should this happen? I'm trying my best, but no matter what I do people still dislike me."

Now, this has nothing to do with the question of my racial attitude. I haven't found that my relations with white people have changed, except that I have gone through, now, some of the experiences which perhaps a white liberal would go through when he doesn't know whether to own up to his black brother or not. In one instance it happened when I tried to get some of the young white Americans here involved in part of the national

cultural celebrations that I was helping to arrange. Tan-
zanians indicated to me that the presence of these young
whites wasn't desirable. I had thought I could use their
services at some of these celebrations, but it was indicated
to me that they just weren't wanted. So then I had to go to
these white people and say, "Well, I'm afraid you just can't
be there." There was a certain reversal of roles.

It is also true that it is a definite disadvantage to me at
times to associate with white Americans. Often I have to
make up my mind, "Well, I will just operate as an
individual and I will accept certain people as my friends,
even though it may hurt me, if I think it's worthwhile."
The roles are definitely reversed.

Q: *Would you come to Africa if you were doing it all
over again?*

Coming to Africa has been very exciting, very stimulat-
ing. There have been a lot of heartbreaks, but most of that
was caused by my own blindness. And much more than the
heartbreaks has been the feeling of definitely being a part
of something which is ongoing, alive and moving. Who
wants to stop being part of a new, moving, experimental
society and go back to where people spend most of their
time watching television or going to the movies? It raises a
real question about a country like America—or the Soviet
Union, for that matter—whether this drive for materialistic
gain is going to mean happiness.

Q: *What advice would you give to an Afro-American
who's coming out here to live?*

I think I would say that any person who wants to come
out to Africa owes it to Africa and to himself not to
idealize but to be very, very hardheaded. He should examine the place he wants to go to very carefully and realize
that people are going to be people, with a lot of the same
failings. But, in addition, he must be ready to "identify"

with the African. He can't come out here and not "leave home." And if he thinks he's going to come here and somehow get a better life quickly, he might as well forget about it because he cannot expect to get rich quick or live at the same economic level as at home. If material things are all-important to him, he shouldn't come because he will be very unhappy and bitter.

Lastly, he has to put himself in perspective in order to realize that what may happen to him here, because of the *history* of the country, is not a personal affront. That's a very important thing. For example, if he were to go to West Africa even with the best intentions in the world, he would find certain kinds of suspicion and hostility. That suspicion and hostility must always be looked on as the result of actions that took place long before he came. So if he thinks, therefore, that the people don't trust *him* or are hostile toward *him,* he's going to be very unhappy. I suppose he should also have a sense of adventure; be willing to go along with a certain kind of experimentation in living. This is a frontier in a way and there's not going to be air conditioning in every place.

Did I ever tell you about one of my friends from the States who came down and went to stay at the Ambassador Hotel in Accra? I went to see him and he was tremendously agitated about the room and I said, "What's the matter?" And he said: "The air conditioning isn't working and I'm bringing up the engineer to find out what's wrong." So I told him, "Look, man, the air conditioning is fine, it's the *air!*"

There *are* people who have been here for many years who identify with Africans by the way they wear their hair, by the way they dress, the things they put in their homes, who *do* identify with African aspirations. There are others who haven't been here who have an idealized picture of what life here is and what Africa's all about, and to them it would be quite a jolt.

Those who knew Richard Wright, who came seeking his own salvation in Africa, say he was putting too much of a burden on the country. One can't expect a country to solve a problem that is a personal one. If one is seeking a psychological home, then one may automatically project upon that country the home one seeks. But if it doesn't answer his need, that doesn't mean that the *country* is lacking.

EUROPE

Reri Grist:

ZURICH

If any single occupation is to be found with more frequency than others among black Americans resident in Europe, it is perhaps that of the operatic singer. In Hamburg and Spoleto, in Oslo and Prague, the Negro singer has found receptive audiences. He has also found opera houses willing to bestow on the talented black singer a status superior to that enjoyed by his counterpart in the United States. In Germany particularly, Negroes are on the rolls of many of the country's opera companies; indeed, Americans of all colors abound on German stages.

The world of the black operatic singer is something removed from the experience of the Negro expatriate who may be struggling to make it in some more prosaic profession. For one, there is a respect for the musical ability of Americans which leads, in turn, to a readiness to accept them as promising members of opera companies. This is especially true in Germany, whose native opera talent was depleted by World War Two.

Secondly, there is the traditional European respect for the musical artist, which lifts him out of the considerations of color and into a favored category of existence.

Ex-New Yorker Reri Grist has qualities which would beckon to success even if she were not, as she is, gifted with a superb coloratura soprano voice. A petite, caramel-skinned beauty with an infectious laugh and a self-mocking humor, she is the kind of woman whom men want instantly to protect, though her velvety façade masks a steely determination.

At the Salzburg Festival, where I met her, critics praised her performances. From the solid successes she had achieved in a dozen European cities, she swept into Salzburg and soared to new fame. Then in February, 1966, after this interview, she returned briefly to the United States for an honor that was nine European years in the making: a debut with New York's Metropolitan Opera Company.

Reri Grist

Q: *Where do you spend the most time in Europe?*

I consider home—for the moment—Zurich. When I first came to Europe in 1959, I went around to opera houses in Italy, Germany, France, even big Vienna, auditioning— and I received some engagements, but I didn't want to stay in one place. I wasn't that *determined* to sing—*as a career.* After all, I had never been to Europe and I just wanted to *see* it, it was *fun!* Singing was a way of making money and since I *was* bitten by the opera bug I felt the opportunities were greater in Europe because there were many more opera houses there.

Q: *What had you done in the U.S.?*

In the States I had been on the stage since I was a little, little child. I was in choruses on Broadway, and did a little acting; I went to my neighborhood dancing school in Jamaica, Long Island. Like some other people in this business I had a stage-struck mother who wanted me to be famous. It was she who gave me this name: Reri. My mother wanted me to be a dancer like Mistinguett, that kind of thing.

I went to the High School of Music and Art in New York so I had some movement toward music. But I was never serious, I just wanted to get married and have a little white house and a white picket fence. Honestly. Being in the theater was not something I chose, something I *decided* to do. I just didn't know anything else. I learned how to cook and to make my own clothes and go through all the typical procedures of a normal, poor, Depression child. To this day I still don't like to wash dishes, but I love to iron and to get on my knees and scrub floors—when I have to. In this business, it's almost like therapy.

Q: *How did you get your start as a singer?*

While I was in the High School of Music and Art a friend of mine, who was studying voice, asked me to go to a voice lesson with her. So I went. The teacher said, "Why don't *you* sing something?" and being very brash I said "Sure." The woman gave me a lesson right then and there, and I was so fascinated with the fact that I could control something I couldn't touch. You can touch the piano or the violin but you can't touch the voice. The woman said to me, "Look, I think you have something worth developing. Would you like to come take some lessons?" I said I didn't have any money—I was still in high school—but I went home and told my mother. Somehow we scraped together some money. I had a job or I was in some Broadway show at night, I've forgotten which—so I could pay for the lessons.

I went faithfully once a week, which was all I could afford, and the teacher began to get really interested and I more so. We worked strictly technically, not doing songs or preparing programs. I got more and more fascinated with the whole thing and I began to improve.

She made a tape of my voice in the beginning and then showed me the result after a certain time, and it was obvious the woman was giving me something I didn't know I had. I had always done little bits of singing in our neighborhood dancing school but it was really for fun—I wasn't *thinking* about anything like being a professional singer, at least not consciously. After a year I really had no more money and we stopped. A year to the day after we stopped, the woman wrote me a letter and said, "Please come back, because I *know* you have something which can be developed. Pay me whenever you can." I went back and worked with her for about two years without paying her, going like two or three times a week. When I got out of school, I began to realize that I really should start paying this woman some money. I went to Queens College, still following music because music and languages interested me.

I began to win little contests in school. People started talking to me about entering national contests and I did. Then I began to find that I was winning these things! Of course my teacher was very proud. She was really an excellent teacher, who has coached some voices that are fabulous. Some of them have just disappeared. There is one Negro tenor here in Europe—I'll never forgive him, I don't care what he says—with the greatest tenor voice I have ever heard and I have heard the tops today. There's no one who can compete with that man. But he's now a mechanic or something. He didn't continue. Look, if it's not in him, it's not in him but it still is a crime with that God-given talent—it's a terrible waste.

Q: *And so your ascent began then?*

Yes. I began winning the various awards such as the Marian Anderson Award and a Rockefeller grant which helped a lot because we were poor. My father is—first of all, he's blind and he works at a newsstand so he doesn't make very much money and he never did. My mother's a housewife. My brothers and I went through city colleges. Anyway, I began to find that here and there someone had begun to hear of my name. I began to be asked to sing in little places in New York. It was still all something I did for fun; the only jobs I really *asked* for were Broadway jobs where you go running to the chorus auditions that's asking for the job. The last Broadway show I was in was *West Side Story*. I was in the chorus and had a few solos, and a little bit of dancing. I'm not a dancer, but I can *move.*

West Side Story was written by Leonard Bernstein, of course, and something got into me to bug him about listening to me sing. At this point I had developed my voice to the point where I *knew* I could sing music other than that of the theater. I kept pestering him to prove I really could sing something else. So finally he consented and I went to Carnegie Hall between performances, in full make-up and in one of these blond wigs that I used to have to wear, stood up on that stage and did the audition. I sang the aria from the opera for which I have achieved whatever fame I have—Zerbinetta in *Ariadne auf Naxos*.

Bernstein said, "Well, I must bow to you. You *can* sing."

And he engaged me then to sing something with the Philharmonic. Had other Negro singers sung with the orchestra? Oh, yes, Adele Addision, probably the late Lawrence Winters. I don't know who preceded me because I was never really involved in the field. I was just going my own little merry way and I didn't know—to this day I still don't know many singers, I try to make it a point to stay away from opera singers, because I don't like them. They are a little too egotistical for me. Being egotistical helps to a certain degree but I've seen too many of them who, like one very famous singer whom we all know, says, "I'm all dressed up"—in her mink and her ermine and her emeralds—"but I've no place to go!" Well, I don't even want to get to that point. It was all fun to me and I want to try and keep the business stuff mostly fun, if I can. I don't want to lose myself in those notes, because those notes don't warm you.

So Bernstein engaged me and that was the last show I did. After that I started doing singing in Washington Square Park in Greenwich Village and the papers began to notice. It was at this time that I came to Europe.

Q: *You've not indicated that your life in New York was rough. Do you feel it was?*

Did I feel hard knocks in my life in New York? I'm sorry, I didn't. I've been asked that many times by reporters here in Europe because I'm expected to be a professional figure of oppression, but I don't have that feeling.

When you talk about hard knocks, the first thing that jumps into my mind is when I was a kid growing up in Spanish Harlem, 102nd Street and First Avenue, where everything was all mixed up and you fought for your life. I do recall the time a little Puerto Rican girl who was darker than I was called me "nigger," so I went running home to my father. He told me what that child meant and I was *wounded,* terribly wounded; there were things like that but I don't really feel that I've been held down.

Q: *In short, you found your own way of not being affected by ghetto life?*

Perhaps I'm just dense, but it never really bothered me or perhaps it was just that the ghetto that I was in was a really mixed-up ghetto and it didn't matter what you were, you had to get out of it and survive as best you could.

I'll tell you this: I've never had such a feeling of being a *Negro* until I came to Europe where I was made aware of being a Negro because I was a novelty—at the time that I came it was still a novelty here to have a brown skin—I was beautiful to *everybody*—I could feel that awareness and I didn't feel that way in the States; in fact, I never thought about it there. In the States I was never really aware of color, it really didn't matter that much. I knew things went on—my brother couldn't be an altar boy because he was a Negro—things like that. Sometimes they told my father he had to sit in the upper part of the church and we had to sit in the lower part of the church—but it never really *bothered* me, I didn't think about it, it just sort of washed off. When I came here, then I became aware that I *really* was different in my appearance. But where I did feel what I describe as "good old American discrimination" was in Germany where the United States Army had been. I'll never forget being in Frankfurt in 1959. We were about to go in a restaurant and there outside there was a sign saying "white only." You can go into Augsburg and Munich today and you still feel the United States Army's presence. It's there, it's definitely there!

Q: *Is there any legacy of anti-Negro feeling in Germany, stemming from what the Germans were taught about the racial inferiority of Negroes by Hitler?*

I'm in a certain social category. I meet a certain kind of person, people who know how to keep a certain face, you know, I'm in an international crowd but I have heard verbal slips, let's say, on the part of people from various backgrounds, shopkeepers for example. You still hear hatred of the Jews . . . of the Negro not so much because there are not enough of them here to threaten Germans. Among the younger group of people, though I don't meet too many of them, I sense this feeling of bigotry has lessened. Only in the areas where the American Army is stationed have I experienced anything against the *Negro* in Germany, but there is definitely a feeling against the Jews. People make remarks, unconsciously—let's say you're introduced to someone at a party, and then you move off in another direction away from the person to whom you were introduced and someone will say to you, "Why, he's a Jew." Or "He's Jewish." Something like that. Which is always a sign to me that the distinction is still there.

Q: *Why did you choose to settle in Zurich?*

Because Dr. Herbert Graf, who has done a lot of work in America, took over the Zurich Opera House. He is a great believer in the talent in America and he wanted to bring in fresh blood. He brought eleven or seventeen people in with him. In 1960 he offered me the chance to be the first coloratura soprano in the house, to sing everything in the original language, and by this time I had come to like Switzerland. It was like America in that I could have an apartment with all the little conveniences that I, as a person of modest means, had had in the U.S. In America, the poor have appliances Europeans would term luxuries. Also Zurich is a cosmopolitan center. I didn't feel that Zurich was German, Italian, French, but a mixture of everything, and I liked that. I know some people say that Switzerland is dull but I don't find that—I have a swinging time when I go to Zurich. I may be wrong in my impression because I went in, made a big success, and people came to *me*. For others, it may have been different. I've heard that many Americans don't like the Swiss because they are not outgoing but they were to *me*. As I say, I'm a little unique in that people have come to me. Perhaps it's also because I learned the language quickly.

But important as anything else, I *love* the place.

Q: *Where in Europe would you like to finally settle down?*

Well, my first choice would be Paris. I've only been there a few times but I swear I'll never go back there *alone*. Paris is, for me, *love!* Even the little kids are making love and the old people are still in love. So Paris is for me the place to live, although recently I've been looking for a house, not necessarily to settle down now but for the immediate future, and the way I reason it must be in a place from which I can travel easily. Well, that's Zurich, Munich, London.

Q: *Do you feel more feminine, more of a woman, here in Europe?*

I feel I've grown a little more secure in myself through Europe. I felt more womanly here than in the States. First, as I've said, I was "beautiful" all of a sudden. In Italy a peasant kept following us one summer and my escort didn't grab him—you know the Italian men can be just awful—because he realized it was just curiosity. The peasant just came up to me on the street, ran his fingers along my arm and he asked me, "Are you the same color all over?" I said, "Well, yes, I am." And he just went off in a state of wonder. I mean, nobody had paid that kind of compliment to me before. And it went beyond the skin thing; people began telling me I had beautiful eyes or a nice figure. I didn't get that in America. In New York a boy friend once chided me, "You and your hair!" Well, people admire my hair here. The boy in New York kept saying he liked straight hair—and since my hair is not straight I used to feel badly about that. How often has my mother said to me: "Marry an Indian." Why? So our children would not have that "hair problem"!

Q: *What about the attitude of European males to women of any color?*

There's a different kind of treatment. The American man—particularly the American Negro—wants to be king, nothing else, boom—just like that. The American non-Negro I haven't had too many experiences with, but my girl friends say it's all "Share fair and square." The European male is different. (Although I get very mad at them because when they get to be about thirty-eight or forty, they start looking for a nineteen- or twenty-two-year-old mistress!) Nevertheless he treats his woman another way. He has more respect for her, he wants to be master, too— he *must* be master—but not in such a way that she's made to feel that she is dirt because he exalts her, too. I know most males would like to be dominant but I think the European male *is* not only more the master but he also has more charm, he has more *savoir-faire*. I think they know how to treat a woman in a way that she appreciates much more than American men do.

Q: *Can an American Negro woman explore all avenues of her personality in America?*

I think she is hampered less by the fact that she is a woman than by the fact that she is a Negro. But I still think she can do it. I gather things are opening up, from what I read, and from what I learn from people coming here, Negroes I've talked to briefly who've come here, there's a quality, there's more strength. I still think you have to plow through a lot of things but it is less now.

Q: *Are you interested in singing back in America?*

Oh, yes. I still feel I'm an American although I'm in Europe. But I'm going through a big thing now at having to go back shortly for engagements. I don't want to go back. I'm very comfortable here. I have a better pace here. When I get to San Francisco, it's going to be a big social whirl, I know it. It is the only city in America in which I could possibly—*possibly*—in the far future, live. When I get into New York, I'm a nervous wreck. I like to go in and go out. As soon as I get out of the airport and I see all those buildings and the heat rising, I start choking up. I feel *scared* in New York, I'm frightened in New York. Everything is so fast, and I feel everyone is so *hip*, there's such a danger! I often feel people are going to do something—or something that *I* say might be misunderstood. I just have to get out of New York! For me to walk the area in which I grew up, now I'm *scared!!* I just don't want to get off the plane, even though I'm happy with my family and I love seeing my parents and my brothers. But I can't make it. I tighten up and I don't relax until I get on the plane again to leave.

Q: *Does that tension affect your singing?*

It doesn't in San Francisco but it has in Chicago. I don't like Chicago at all and I know I didn't sing as well there as I can. It is another cold, dirty, and—in another style—fast and dangerous town. When I took a taxi there to the airport the Negro cab driver was talking to me and I didn't know what he was talking about—it was like a foreign language. He had the sort of accent that I've heard people imitate—a Southern ignorant sort of person speaking, but yet something belonging to the Negro—you know, the kind of speech used by Hattie MacDaniel in films—and I couldn't understand *anything!* I felt embarrassed, because this was a black man and I am also one of him and he of me, but I felt—well, I was sorry and I was ashamed.

Q: *Do you feel any guilt about not being there at this time in the struggle of the Negro?*

No, I don't, I really don't. I was recently talking to dancer Arthur Mitchell, and Arthur said Harry Belafonte had been criticizing him, saying "You don't march" to protest and all that. Arthur told Harry, "Look, anybody over twelve is hopeless. I work with the *kids!*" Well, I don't even do that, but I don't feel guilty. I'll send money to the NAACP because we've always done that since we were children—send your little dime—and my brother is very active in community affairs, a real flag-waver for the Negro cause—but I don't feel *Negro!* I feel that I don't belong anywhere, yet I get mad when I read about Selma, because it's unjust, but I can't identify myself there. Maybe it's because I've been rejected a lot by Negroes. In fact I was always considered by the kids in the neighborhood a snob because I didn't talk the way they did. The Negro kids who were in *West Side Story,* always used to say, "Oh, who in the hell does she think she is, so high hat?" I mean, I can't *sing* spirituals. I was laughed out of a Negro church trying to sing spirituals—I was trying to give all my heart to what I thought was the Negro spiritual and they laughed me out of the church.

Q: *What would you say to any other American Negro coming to Europe?*

That depends on what they are coming away from. And what they think they are going to find here. I remember vague faces in Paris in 1959, the so-called Negro exiles, who didn't escape anything. They brought it with them and they were still struggling with the effects of all the mistreatment and the ideas engrained in them in the

States. They brought the "Negro problem" to Europe. Leaving didn't solve anything for them. In this respect, I agree with James Baldwin. He says he came to Paris and he thought it was all over, but it wasn't all over. It was in *him* and he had to deal with *him* first! And the only way he could do it was to go back. And from the way he writes, he's gotten over it, but it was in *him*. Paris was not going to relieve him of it.

Some people can function well with the kind of tension being a Negro in America generates. Take Miles Davis. I know Miles has so much hatred in him that when he's really mad, Miles will stand up and play his heart out. But I don't think I ever get mad because of the color thing and I'm better off without the pressures of race. I will confess this: When I appeared at the Salzburg Festival in 1964 (I think the only other Negroes who had been in Salzburg were Leontyne Price, who caused quite a sensation with her beautiful voice, and Grace Bumbry), I felt a responsibility to the Negro people to do all I could, as a performer who happened to be a Negro—that night. I can't go through the logic of why, where it comes from and all that. I had that feeling—but I'll never have it again. Walking through the streets, I'm relaxed here. If I want to go out in sneakers and with my hair not straightened, I can do so and not feel ashamed because I'm a Negro. I may feel ashamed because I don't make such a nice picture and I'm aware of people staring at me, but I don't feel strange because I'm a *Negro*.

I think I've done very well here and from the reaction of the people during the two years I've sung the same parts, I have come to realize that I have reached an international position and that I could compete musically with anybody anywhere today—in my category.

I'm not in Zurich much any more; in order to work

there you have to do a certain number of performances. I still have my apartment but I will only be doing six performances there. Now I sing everywhere. Where am I going to live? Now, don't get on that subject! I don't know yet. The time has come when I feel within me that perhaps I've done enough traveling. But I still don't know where I'll live permanently.

Art Simmons:

PARIS

*The sound of jazz as played by another black Ameri-
can, in-group Negro humor, the familiar backdrop of
black accents are all part of a quality of life which the
black expatriate occasionally seeks out to water the roots of
his being. In night spots like the Folk Studio in Rome or
restaurants like the Drop Inn in Copenhagen, black folk—
resident and transient—turn up to mingle, tell a tale or
two, and renew old ties. In Paris, the Living Room, 25 rue
du Colisée, is such an oasis. It is a favorite command post
for American Negroes passing through Paris—especially
jazz musicians—but is popular with French jazz aficio-
nados, too. At the Living Room, Art Simmons is both host
and a permanent fixture at piano leading his combo.
Simmons is a man of medium build with café au lait skin,
prominent cheekbones, an infectious laugh, and the con-
vivial pianist is the chief reason for the popularity of the
Living Room. Whether he is hovering over his keyboard,*

*floating gentle ballads out into the dimly lit room, or
bantering with visitors like Sidney Poitier or Joe Louis,
Simmons seems to be enjoying himself immensely and
somehow the relaxed* ambiance *communicates itself to his
auditors.*

*The Living Room is also a good place to find out who's
in town, who just left town, to pick up a message or to
leave one for somebody else. Simmons keeps a file of
addresses that may not always surface the person you are
seeking but will at least usually get you started on your
way to your quarry. But mostly the Living Room is just a
warm sanctuary for those who want a little soulful jazz and
a relaxed joint to hear it in.*

Art Simmons

I've been living in Paris since 1949. I came to
Europe in 1946 with the Army's Special Service Band in
Germany. I was twenty years old then. Home in the States
was West Virginia where I went through West Virginia
State College and later Bluefield State College. I came
directly from West Virginia to Europe.

Although I came to Paris to study, I guess in the back of
my mind I knew I wanted to stay. West Virginia as a place
was more liberal than other Southern states, but there are
few opportunities there for white or colored.

The piano was for me a means of survival; I was
basically an arranger, so I went to the Paris Conservatory
for a year, then I was at the Ecole Normale for three years.
My French is "bedroom French." . . . I couldn't speak
the language when I came but I manage to get by now

without any problems. My French would have been better if I had stuck with French girls, but along the way I got involved with about three American girls, and an English one, too—you know, let's face it, you hear all this stuff about "Negroes like white women." Hell, I like *pretty women!* Period. If she's Icelandic or whatever and good looking I'm going to have to go along!

There are some colored guys here who are living on the fringes, guys who'll con anybody—and you've got to watch them. They'll use anything to get ahead—"Negroism" or anything else. They come here under the guise of intellectualism but, man, they're phonies. It doesn't take long to see through all that talk. You watch them and after about a week ask yourself, "What does he do? What does he *really* do?" He says he's a writer or he's a painter, but you don't see any writing or any painting and after a while people put him down—it doesn't take long. As soon as you arrive, people try to find out whether you're married, whether you're "gay" or exactly where you're at.

Q: *Is there some reason why the guys here tend not to have French girls but rather English, American and such?*

Oh, I think that's just chance. Some of it's language, of course. I'd like to point out that there's a big fallacy about French chicks. There's this Playboy myth—Americans come over here expecting all sorts of things out of French women, but all the things you hear these stories about are really about whores. To get a good French girl from a good French family is hard, harder than in the States, that I know. How many girls do you see around this club unescorted?

The authorities are very lenient here. For example, after fifteen years residence here I've only just got my working papers. But I was producing and giving Frenchmen work and the French respected that. I've always worked with a couple of French boys in my group. I'm intelligent enough to know I'm not going to come here and bring in an all-American trio—after all, this is *their* country. They could have kicked me out of here a long time ago, don't think they didn't know that. They know all about you. You always have to have your passport—wherever you live, the concierge has to declare you—they know where you are from the time you come in at the airport!

There are some pathetic aspects to this Paris thing. If you only knew how many Negro girls have come here because they found out that Josephine Baker was a big star here. Many of these girls who couldn't make it in the States but figured they could come over here and make it. But man, the war is over! It's no longer a novelty to be a Negro in Paris. That's all finished now. They've seen good, they've seen bad—you have to *produce* as a performer. Before, you were a Negro first. Now you are a Negro second.

I learned French in order to get over a complex: I'm naturally a little timid. I'm timid about walking into a strange place. The most beautiful thing that's happened to me here is that now I realize when I walk in somewhere and people look at me, it may be because I'm good looking! I never thought of that back in the States; I just knew it was because I was Negro.

You know, to be honest, I'm very race-conscious, anybody who knows me knows that, but it's in a positive sort of way. How many races have produced an Art Tatum? Or a Duke? The sophistication, the beauty we've got. . . . I know the beauty of my race. Look at all the beautiful people who have come out of this rough-hewn rock, because many of us haven't had the benefit of education. Yet look at Negro spirituals, the quality, the beauty of them, the pure beauty!

There is no Negro "community" here as such. I don't know why. But there is a tendency for musicians to hang out with other musicians. *I* don't, because I find most of them are a bore. I know more music than the average one of them, so I can't talk music with them. I hang out mostly with writers and painters from whom I can learn something and some of the other musicians do, too.

Just because we all know each other doesn't mean we're a community. I know many of the white Americans here too. But, at the same time, don't think we Negroes don't make it our business to know where we all are. I guess that's kind of a safety valve to have in case something goes wrong. After all, why do I buy *Ebony* Magazine over here? Because I want to know what my people are doing, that's why. I guess we *are* a community but not a *visual* community. We need each other—and we call on each other. When we first come here, we're told to contact each other. If I come knowing someone here I can easily find out where to contact him. I suppose there *is* a community! Even though we're all over town, we all know where to come to meet other Negroes: the three restaurants, Haynes', Gaby's, and Bill Baskerville's.

There are two or three civil rights groups among Afro-Americans in Paris. They've got SNCC *—they gave a benefit and I played for them. By *law,* we were not allowed to make that civil rights march that we held at the U.S. Embassy last year. The French cops put that sort of thing under the heading of "politics" and said if we wanted to demonstrate, "Go back there and do it!" But a lawyer got them to let us march if we would stay seventy-five yards apart, and it was a beautiful thing, very dignified. It started right out from the Living Room Club here on a Friday afternoon. During a visit to Europe once, Martin

* The Student Non-Violent Coordinating Committee.

Luther King said, "The Negro over here is an enigma." He was right. I don't care how I try to rationalize my being here, I know I belong there. But I am selfish enough as an artist to want to stay here, you know what I mean, I have got to live for myself. Let's be honest about it—I'm very "Negro" but I'm also very "me."

It doesn't matter whether you're a Negro or what, you're still an individual. I've met Negroes who come over here and act like real asses. Don't think I don't tell them, "Look, I live here. Let's not come over here and ruin it!"

Two Cats
and a Conversation:

PARIS

Europe for many a black man is a place of self-discovery, but it is a revelation arrived at slowly. In the black ghettos of America, Negroes examine their dilemma as if it were an onion, peeling back layer after layer until the essence of their condition is revealed in a pungent kernel.

Sometimes it happens that two black compatriots live in the same area, look at the same conditions, arrive at the same general conclusions about their destinies, but never communicate their agonizing analyses to each other. Perhaps because the introspection, the analysis of the data, the weighing of alternatives goes on almost unconsciously until that day when the mental meter reads "enough" and the internal alien begins packing his bags.

Daniel L. Johnson is a 27-year-old painter now resident

in Paris. Henry C. Carr, 28, is a businessman whose base is Rome. Both are black and grew up as friends in the same Los Angeles neighborhood. In America, neither talked to the other about leaving the country of their birth, but somehow both wound up in Europe.

Recently they met in Paris to which Danny Johnson had just come to take up a foundation grant and through which Henry Carr, who has lived in Europe for more than a year, was passing on his way back to Los Angeles for a visit.

It was a time for renewing old ties, exchanging impressions and for examining the nature of the black American outside his native habitat. The following conversation with the editor grew out of this reunion.

Two Cats and a Conversation

JOHNSON: He and I went to the same grammar school, lived ten blocks from each other in Los Angeles, saw each other regularly. So he's in Europe for *his* reasons and I for mine, and we run into each other here! I hadn't seen you in, how long?

CARR: I can't remember, but I have been in Europe now fourteen months and maybe once or twice on trips back home I'd run into you.

Q: *How long ago did you think about coming here?*

CARR: All my dreams started about Europe back in Los Angeles in tenth grade. When the high school seniors graduated each summer, some cats would go to Europe. After they came back they'd talk about what they got into, how beautiful the European experience was, and they'd compare what was happening here to what was going on in America.

Q: *What kind of a school was it?*

JOHNSON: Oh, it was a "nice" high school. And integrated. When I went there, there were more whites enrolled than there were Negroes. Later I was the first Negro to get a full scholarship to Chouinard Art Institute, which knocked me into an all-white situation. There were only two Negroes in the whole school along with about five hundred whites and Orientals. It was sort of like being in Europe, philosophically. The other students didn't know anything about me and the only relationships we had were through art—we talked about what we believed in, what we thought we could do. Then summertime would come around, man, and since these white kids were middle-class or better, *they'd* go to Europe. Then they came back, talking about how much Europe had it over America, but from a completely *white* viewpoint. So there *I* was, with my poor financial status, trying to figure out how *I* was going to cut loose from all that so I could be more white, because that's exactly what it was! I wanted what everyone else had. There are a few things I enjoy that are automatically *status quo* here and elsewhere in Europe, things that do not exist for Negroes at home. So in a sense it is like being white here, which is ironic.

CARR: What he means is over here you feel like a real human being and you know the value of your own work and are able to see what it can be, whereas in the States, they don't allow you to see it that way.

Now, I'm not saying there is no kind of bias here. If a person goes to an Italian factory and he's an Italian, he'll generally get priority because it's *his* country. But that isn't any discrimination.

JOHNSON: What has been important to me is this hang-up of pressure, this constant feeling of—you know—"I'm a Negro . . . he's screwing with me or he will screw with me, so be cool, be careful." Like the thing with the house today. Supposedly the American Embassy helped me rent a house. I went to see the man who was handling the house for the proprietor. When I got there, the cat rented me the place and that was that. But what he was *supposed* to do was notify the actual owner in England that there was somebody to rent the house and then the owner would come over and take care of the business, look me over and all that kind of thing.

So I'm sitting in my house yesterday and all of a sudden the door opens up with a key and in walk these people and they say, "Who are you?" and I say, "Who are you?" I said, "I'm the one that's renting the house," and they said, "You are? We didn't know anything about it. Who signed the papers?" I said, "Well, here's my receipt," and all this crap. These people were just shocked, you know, because we'd taken their drawers and underwear and just thrown them in a closet. She was all worked up about her personal things. So I went to the Embassy this morning and I told them what's happening and they said, "Oh yes, we heard from Mr. Charlay, the owner. He called and said he was coming in." (That was the cat who came back from England and who owns the house.) So he's at the Embassy right now and I'm supposed to go there after this. I don't know what crap he talked about. But they collected my rent and the cat that owns the house called my wife to ask, "Is everything all right? Are you settled in the hotel? Don't worry about anything." Mistakenly, *I* had thought he was trying to screw me up! You see it was that "Negro thing" again. Now I know it was just their mistake. If I had moved up in the Fairfax neighborhood in L.A., my assumption would not have been wrong. You know, the cat might say, "Yeah, Danny, here's the key," and I'd move in but the next pressure that comes along, I'm out. It doesn't seem to be happening like that here. I won't know until I talk to the cat. I called him up and told him my furniture was coming and he said, "Don't worry about it, it's all right," but see, the thing that threw me is *why* is he comin' to the Embassy today?

CARR: Well, they do that. If a guy doesn't have a job, a prospective landlord is concerned about your means. In a way I can understand that.

I had an experience when I came here to Paris. My roommate and I had driven about twenty hours and we were grubby and dirty. We were looking for a hotel and we couldn't find anything. I went to this real nice hotel and asked for a room there. The clerk looked us up and down and said, "I don't know if we have any rooms," and all the time he's looking at *me*—because my roommate's Italian. So I said, "Look, I don't want to stay here. This cat's looking me up and down as if I don't belong here or as if I can't afford to stay here."

This was in Paris. So I said, "Let's go." And the desk guy says, "No, no, no, no, Monsieur."

At the next hotel they almost did the same thing, but then they saw the car we pulled up in and so there was all kinds of service. My friend stayed with me for two days and then he left and went back to America. When he left, he didn't check out of the hotel so the next day the manager of my hotel called me down and said, "Well, what about your friend, he didn't pay his bill." I told him to put the bill on my bill and I would take care of it. He looked at me as if he were wondering, "What kind of a spook are *you?*"

Some girls that I know from Rome, who happen to be white, are in town. They came to visit me and since two of them don't have bags or rooms I told them, "Yes, take a bath in my place." And they stayed all day and I guess these hotel people don't know what the hell is happening! Every time I walk out of that hotel, the elevator man and the man at the door give me these looks like you wouldn't believe.

JOHNSON: I'll tell you what was really strange, man *strange*. I drove all the way from Los Angeles to New York by an extreme northern route with my wife and my kids. My wife is part Italian and part Spanish. That trip was like a living nightmare every time I stopped. But I never had any incident except one time in Indiana, South Bend, Indiana. They said, meaning the Negro part of town, "Your hotel's down there," and I said, "Well, turn off your motherf——— 'vacancy' lights then."

CARR: Now to me, there are shades of prejudice, I don't care where you go. The entire summer, May through August, I traveled here in Europe. I went to Athens, I went to Yugoslavia, I went to Spain, Germany, I just traveled all over. I never really did have any trouble. When I first came to Rome, this is all I thought of, you know, that I'd walk into a place and they would look at me and have a reaction. But after four or five months, after I knew the Italian mentality, I didn't feel any pressures at all. I felt just like an Italian and I'd forgotten about America completely. No feeling for it at all.

The white man comes to Europe, the white Southerner, especially, and when he sees a Negro walking with a white girl he still frowns at it, whereas the European doesn't say anything. It's just two people walking by.

JOHNSON: Oh, yeah, the white American that comes over here, he still is very strong on that.

Q: *When you see a white face here, how do you react?*

CARR: Nothing, it means nothing to me, it meant nothing in America.

JOHNSON: He used to be with the Sammy Davis crowd. He was always up there in Hollywood. He lived near where we lived but he was always up there.

CARR: When I graduated from high school I was the only Negro in my class who went to UCLA or went to a university, *period!* When I got to college I met a whole new circle of friends. I didn't join a Negro fraternity, I went around with a group of kids who had certain things. So I had nothing in common with my peer groups whom I'd grown up with. I was friendly with them but as far as socializing with them goes, that had stopped. I was a political science major in college. First I wanted to apply for a scholarship to come to Europe to study the political situation but after I graduated I went into public relations and I worked for the Los Angeles Board of Education in their TV department. I worked there for about eight months and I was on the verge of getting married but you know, this whole Negro question was beginning to drive me crazy. I got to where I said, "I can't take it any more." And I started saving my money to leave.

The girl that I was engaged to was a model. Her mother was a doctor up in San Francisco, a very prominent woman, but somewhat unrealistic as far as what Negroes were and what they should be. Her whole thought pattern was white. But her daughter could marry me because she thought I lived in that same world and thought like she thought. So she accepted me, but then it got to where her mother was ordering, "You live in this type of house," "You buy this type of furniture!" "You do this," "You do that." I didn't want it like that. But my girl was abiding by what her mother wanted her to do.

It was something that I didn't want to be a part of, plus, I think, too, that I never really felt that in Los Angeles I could get the status I wanted in public relations as a

Negro. I really didn't see any future in what I was involved in. For example, I had been in a program with twelve white guys who were the same type of guy as I was. We were directed to different channels where we could enhance what we had learned in school. And of the white boys, one was sent to Warner Brothers, one went to the William Morris Agency, both top organizations. But not me. I felt, well, hell, that I had broke my ass and done much more than these cats ever did and what I had done or what I was really interested in didn't mean anything because I was a Negro.

Then I thought I would try in Europe and see what was there. I figured I'd get some experience in Europe, go back to America, establish myself, and then make a life of it. But now after living in Rome for over a year, I see it completely differently. Now I'm going home briefly only to see my family. There are three of us—the other two are white Americans—who are opening a club in Rome. This is a whole new thing for me. I have a sort of sponsor who is also helping me out.

Q: *What do you feel when you go into a new situation, both in America and here?*

CARR: There are places where I have gone in California with white friends, in Balboa for instance, that cater to the upper-crust white American Protestant. I remember my girl and I went to a restaurant there once with a white boy and his girl. He happened to meet some friends outside and he said he'd join us shortly. I didn't think that any trouble was possible because my whole living situation was completely beyond any thought of that. You know, I felt I was completely accepted like they were. I didn't think any different at all. My girl and I walk into the restaurant and the maître d' calls us and says, "No, no" and I thought maybe there wasn't any room but I looked around the place and saw lots of empty tables. So I said, "What's wrong?" and he said, "Well, I'm sorry, you can't stay here." I began to walk out. My friend walked up and said, "What's wrong?" and I didn't want to upset him because he had gone on so about this place, about how he knows the owner and it being so good and all that. The maître d' came up then and says, "Are these friends of yours?" I said, "Yeah." Then he said to me, "Well, you can have everything on the house," and I said, "I don't want it, I don't want a ———— thing you have." Only when I came across situations like that would I react.

Then I would go to Palm Springs for the week end. Palm Springs was almost the same thing. They have a lot of Negroes down there but the Negroes are all servants. When I went down there, I was always staying at somebody's house or going to a spa bath with the group. So no one ever said anything, but I'm sure if I'd gone on my own, it would have been a completely different scene.

JOHNSON: You see, I didn't have the courage. I had white friends because I went to an all-white school, but I never made it socially with them. Only once a year would I mingle with them socially and that was at graduation. I always knew if I did, someone would grin or screw up and say the wrong thing and I would explode, so I avoided it. I never got involved. But you see, there's one thing: I never had the opportunity to meet people on the same kind of level he did, and the kind of business he is in is a little bit different from the kind of field that I'm in. For one thing, among the people who are in drama and have made it or will make it, there's sort of an understood thing that "this cat has paid dues and he is no longer the ordinary kind of Negro"—you know—"he's in with us." That is, among white theatrical people.

CARR: I was in Majorca once. My associates and I had

gone there to look for a possible business venture. Majorca has a population of 290,000. Ten thousand are Majorcan. The rest are foreigners. Twenty thousand German, a very large British population, Americans and Swedes. The first couple of days there I saw practically no black faces at all, and I noticed that because of this being such a tourist resort, the tourists had caused a conflict within the Spaniards' own feelings about blacks. Their whole treatment was so vague . . . not really unkind, but it wasn't what I felt that the Greeks had shown me. In Yugoslavia—I couldn't believe it, it was so great. You know, the same Socialist country we frown on in America. We drove through the town and the people followed us, they almost bowed to us. Actually, it was almost too much for me to take.

In Germany I felt the Germans were very good, you know, as far as *I* was concerned. First of all there are many Fulbright students here. Mainly Negro girls who are studying opera. Negro actors who *can* get parts here. Nothing great, but when there's work they can get it. And they can live on what they get.

JOHNSON: (after telephone call with owner of house he is renting, who confirms the rental) : You see, *that's* the kind of thing I *never,* in my whole life, in America, experienced. Here I am thinking that I'm about to be evicted by these owners and then I call and I get, "Oh, yes, Mr. Johnson, we just came in to check on you and see if you were financially able to pay." The owners had merely come back so that they could move their things out of there! I guess they think I'm rich.

CARR: Every African I've met in Rome has been just filthy rich and because some Africans are wealthy many Romans assume that *all* Negroes are in the same category. They respect them so now they treat me like an African, but who cares? What's wrong with being an African? I'm just beginning to be proud of this heritage, whereas before, since the white man always taught us in school that they were such savages, I would say, "No, uh-uh, I have no African blood." I would *make up* a blood rather than admit it.

There are plenty of Negroes in Rome who go "West Indian," who say, "No, I don't know nothin' about *Negro.*"

JOHNSON: I would never do that. I always want whites to know, wherever I am, that *I* come from America.

CARR: I don't give a damn what the European thinks, that I'm a black Frenchman or an African or anything. I just want him to treat me as if he were my brother, you know, the same type of respect for my dignity, for what I feel, for my worth as a human being. Be treated like there's just one race. I can't say I've found that completely in Europe because I'd be lying, but it's the closest thing I've found to democracy and to the liberal type of freedom that we talk about in America. They talk about it in Los Angeles too, but yet the Watts thing happens. I was shocked to hear about it. Take the neighborhood where my family is living. We moved there four or five years ago. The first week we were there, every tire on our car was slashed. They took ink and mud and threw it over our fence. And then, two years after we moved in, another Negro family moved in, a jazz musician. And they bombed his house. He lived around the corner from us in View Park, Los Angeles. But now, you know, hell, it's nothing like that now.

JOHNSON: Remember when you used to ride your bike up through there when you were a kid? And all the old white cats, the retired cats that owned that section, they'd go wild, man.

CARR: I don't know if our neighbors are still like that, but I know that when I left we had never yet spoken to our neighbors and we had been there five years. They would call the police when I gave big parties and had a band. They'd see these girls coming in, white girls, Japanese girls, everything. They'd see this and they couldn't imagine what was happening and they'd call the police.

Two days before I left I had a big dinner and I had Sammy Davis there and he invited his friends and they came up in their Rolls-Royces and then the day after that, our neighbor spoke. But his wife has never said a word yet. And I would break my back. I would speak and these people wouldn't say a damn word. I'd say, "Hello, Mr. and Mrs. Smith," and they wouldn't even smile.

Do you know the Varioli section of Rome? It's the residential section, a very posh section. When I moved into that area, not knowing what the Italians are like, I had an Italian friend get the place for me—only because he could get it cheaper, not because I was a Negro. I wound up paying eighty dollars a month for an apartment that an American ordinarily would have paid two hundred dollars for. It was unbelievable. No American could have gotten this place. It was, you know, like a villa, with a huge garden, trees all over, three bedrooms, I had a big party room—a real European pad. It was beautiful. And when I first moved in there were no Negroes living in the area. I bought a dog and I'd walk my dog and they'd look at me and they'd look at my dog and they'd snicker and smile, but it wasn't the type of thing that I'd known in the States . . . they weren't being vindictive at all. I knew this, but at first I didn't understand because I'd go sit on my piazza to have coffee and they'd come up to me and want to take my picture. I said no, because then I didn't know they were doing it just because they were curious.

JOHNSON: But it's been a whole metamorphosis for both of us.

CARR: I'm going home now for two months because I'm going into business in Italy and who knows when I'll go back home again. I don't really want to go back.

I'll tell you what happened to a Negro friend of mine —who had lived in Europe five years—which was shattering to him. He left Rome and went to Los Angeles because his mother was sick. He got off the airplane. He was the only one in customs who had his every bag gone through; they detained him for one hour, *for one hour!* You know, after living in Europe and not knowing—because a Negro in Europe after a while forgets how it is back there—once again he was a black face who had no worth, just "a nigger." He had planned to stay the summer, but after two weeks he came back to Rome.

JOHNSON: Well, you know, you have a very interesting point there and I'm glad that you mentioned it first. In my mind, there is a diabolical plan in America to keep Negroes screwed up psychologically. Like I was. Once you come here and you're part of this, you look back, baby, and you see all *hinds* of things, like, take the hippest Negro that you knew in L.A. What is he? What does he talk about? About something predicated on financial gain, a flashy woman, a big house or car, a real "tough" apartment and a good "tough" job. That's his game, that's his whole scheme! He never talks about the basic things, like a policeman saying "Bonjour, m'sieur" to you on the street.

CARR: In New York or anywhere in America you can't stop and get the courtesy that we get here. In Italy if I were speeding and they'd stop me here, they'd talk and explain.

JOHNSON: But the white European who goes to America becomes "white."

CARR: I agree with that.

JOHNSON: When the white European makes it to America he does either of two things. They either come back revolted because of the oppression they have seen, the way Negroes live in squalor in New York City—they just don't understand that and they just don't want to hear or accept what Americans have to say about it—or they become "white," the kind of biased person you and I have confronted all our lives.

Q: *Have you met the* pied-noir, *the French settlers from Algeria who are like the Southern rednecks?*

CARR: This is where I got very involved with the Africans. I have never been so impressed and so taken aback because, you know, I'd never even *thought* of Africans in any way at all. Like I said, I had one idea in my mind because of what the white man had taught us about the Africans as savages. Then I met all of these educated, intellectual Africans who have studied in London and Paris, who are so far above us it's ridiculous. I saw this and thought, "What American crap is this they've tried to feed us about Africans being savages?" It's sick.

Personally, I don't want any part of it any more. Maybe I'm a weakling, maybe it boils down to this: maybe I'm trying to escape from something. But in the final analysis I don't really think that is true because for the first time in my life I've been completely happy—as a Negro. I can walk down the street, look in a window, go into a store, go into a restaurant, and know that I can stay there as long as I have the money to pay my bill. I'm treated just like the next man. This to me is a beautiful feeling.

Q: *Do you feel a need to see other Negroes?*

CARR: Oh, yeah, it occurs, it does. When I first got here I'd see Negroes in Rome and I'd try to talk to them because I knew I could *communicate* with these people without a whole lot of jazz. I felt the brotherhood . . . and these Negroes, they wouldn't *allow* it because they figured I thought I was better than they, because I had just come from the States. But I do feel there is a definite need for Negroes in Europe to get together. Not all the time, because a Negro who has lived in Europe forgets race and begins to become an individual. He makes friends because of what he feels about a specific person. But still there comes a point where the Negro wants to get together and have that finger-popping session and be able to talk about the chitlins and the greens and everything else.

JOHNSON: I don't think I know yet whether it's important. I *do* know the greatest thing I can hope for is to run into a partner from home, a school chum. There's no linguistic difficulty, it's "home." That kind of thing I always want to have a rapport with. Now I am not necessarily concerned with *seeking out* Negroes, but if I feel like it I can always go to Gaby's soul food restaurant here and talk to the cook who has a Southern French accent—an American Negro from the South but with a French accent. He speaks the language fluently, and he tells me, "Yeah, baby, every time I pick up a paper, it ain't better *yet!*"

Edward Barnett:

PARIS

There is a Paris most American visitors never see. It
is not in the Michelin Guide nor is it mentioned in tourists' letters back home. It is the world of those expatriates,
black and white, who are employing every scheme, dodge
and hustle known to Western man to survive in the City of
Light. It is a world bordered by the temporarily flush
friend whose "ship has just come in" and the woman tourist determined not to go back to Cincinnati without that
one kind of sexual experience she had not dared indulge in
Ohio.

It is a daily round of jagged uncertainties, in which
black con men rush from café to snack bar to bistro seeking
that action, whatever comes, that will snare enough elusive
francs for another meal, a bottle of wine, a thin wedge of
insulation against the chill specter of a vagrancy arrest and
deportation. They live at the other end of the line from
the well-fed opera singers, the respected professors, the

*coddled GI's. Yet theirs, too, is the realm of the black ex-
patriate, these Negroes who came to the Continent with no
diplomas, no special skills except the mental survival kits
constructed in Watts, Hough, Harlem and a dozen other
American ghettos.*

*A few brave souls, living on the frontiers of poverty,
manage to resist the pull of the Parisian netherworld as
they struggle to implement some private vision. Ed Barnett is one of these. Secreted in a tiny apartment off a
dimly lit courtyard in a working-class section of Paris, Barnett, thirty-five, nurses a dream: to make it as a high-
fashion photographer for the more affluent magazines.
With the encouragement of his beautiful Swedish wife,
Kerstin, and a small circle of American friends who are
also trying to succeed in Paris, Barnett tightropes through
the lean days between assignments, doggedly makes the
rounds of the Parisian slicks. For him, as for many of the
Negroes there, Paris may not yield everything for which he
came to Europe, but it contains more than enough for
which to stay.*

Edward Barnett

I came to Paris on June 13, 1960. I grew up in Detroit. I'd thought about coming for a couple of years. I like
to travel and I'd never been to Europe, so I thought I'd
come over. I had been in the Orient as a soldier during the
Korean War. Actually, I was born in Chicago. After Detroit, I moved to San Francisco.

Q: *Was it hard to come over here?*

No, I just got right up and came.

Q: *Was it a big break?*

No, not really. Not if you have the travel bug. You know, it's just another place to go. I didn't come to *Paris*, mind you, I just came to *Europe*. I toured Europe before I settled here. I went all over the Iberian Peninsula, to Morocco, Italy, Austria, Yugoslavia, Greece, Germany, Belgium, Holland and England on a tour that took a little over two years. I traveled around, using Paris as a base. I toured Southern Europe before I got to Paris. I stayed in Paris here a year, then moved on to other places, just as a tourist.

Q: *How long were you in Yugoslavia?*

Six weeks. I liked the weather down there. The people are very friendly. They are very outgoing, especially in the hinterland where they never have seen any black people. I went to within seven miles of the Albanian border, into these little towns where you know they don't see many black people—but they were friendly and curious.

Q: *And why Paris?*

Well, I told myself that wherever I got my first job, then that's where I'd stay. I came to Paris on June 13, 1960, and I went down to the *New York Herald Tribune* International Edition and got myself a job selling that paper on the street.

Q: *You really tried to look for work elsewhere?*

Yes, in Vienna and in Italy. I went around looking for work. I just wanted to see what it was like, and if I could find a job, not knowing the ropes. I didn't know anybody. Most people that I met on the road, you know, hitchhikers—I stayed in youth hostels most of the time—said that Paris is a hard town to try to work in.

Q: *What sort of thing had you done in the States?*

I worked in a psychiatric clinic in California and at odd jobs while I was going to school. I worked at the post office, drove a bus, worked for the railroad, the usual. I got a job here and so it kept me here, because at that time money had to come in.

Q: *Do you think there's a Negro "community" in Paris?*

There's no ghetto. I would say that there is a thin layer of community feeling, we are all Afro-Americans, we speak the same tongue, we don't have to explain when we use certain colloquialisms. And when you're down and out, you try to help each other—at least *I* do the best I can. We are all kinds, you know, a painter here, a writer there; I'm a photographer. Maybe you can pick up a job through them, you know.

Q: *If another Afro-American comes to Paris to live, is it likely that you will meet him?*

Well, it's according to who he is—if he has a big name, of course, you read about it in the papers.

Q: *I mean any ordinary guy who has just come in.*

No, you just run into them. They'll go to places like Montmartre. And you may see him there. It's according to his personality—if he's an extrovert, he will get around and you may run into him.

Q: *How about this business of making a living when you're not a national of the country?*

Well, let me put it this way, they don't put out any red velvet carpet. You make it or you don't. When you don't make it, it comes down to "no food" and living in the streets, literally. There's a saying here that "if you have friends in Paris you can't go hungry" and that does seem to be relatively true. I haven't really gone hungry yet. But I have lost a little weight in my time.

Q: *Are most of the Afro-Americans you know working?*

Well, yeah. You can't say "most" and you can't say "jobs" because you have to qualify each—if the guy has a skill. I have a friend, for instance, who's in advertising and

he works at it. He works for an English advertising firm. I
have another friend who's working on his doctorate now.
And I'm trying to break into fashion and advertising
photography. There are painters here and they sell their
paintings—that's the way it goes. Then there are the musicians. I think they have it the easiest, in my personal
opinion.

As a photographer I'm competing against French and
American photographers. The general feeling is that the
big magazines in Paris, the big advertising agencies, prefer
American photographers—after all, New York is the heart
of advertising and fashion.

Q: *When you were in the States did you find the racial
problems particularly hard to live with?*

Well, let's put it this way, I didn't realize just how hard
it was to live with until I got out from under it. I felt the
pressure like any black man will, but the thing is you're
born with it and you take it for granted.

Q: *You say you felt pressure there. Did this contribute
to your wanting to see what else was happening in the
world?*

I always had the travel bug even as a kid. But the pressure was there, too; it was something you accepted or
didn't accept but it was there all the time. So you leave,
like I did. Then you have to recondition yourself. In Spain
I ran into an Italian hitchhiking. He said, "Come visit me
when you get to Florence." Now, my mind being American and suspicious, asks: "Does he seriously mean this?"
Well, he really meant it. In the States, you'd say, "He
might or he might not," because nine chances out of ten
he'd just be acting friendly and the invitation wouldn't
really hold. Such small things as that you wouldn't even
think about in the States. I came to the conclusion that a
black man—not only a black man, any man—does not have

to live like that. Over here prejudices exist too. As long as
the white man has his power, there's going to be some degree of it. But the point is that you don't run into it every
day of your life. I learned that after being here a while I
didn't give it that much thought.

Q: *How about the way you related to white people you
met after you came here?*

You mean the conditioned response? When I run into a
Swede or any European, or an Asiatic, I don't have it, but
as soon as I hear that American accent—the conditioning
comes right back. That still hasn't died.

Q: *Did you feel there was any kind of adjustment to be
made to white people in Europe?*

No, I didn't. That was one of the adjustments *I* had to
make. I learned that if a man was friendly toward me in
Europe—a European—he's generally sincere in his friendliness. He may have a lot of misconceptions about me and
my country, but when he extends his hand in friendship
it's honestly extended. And I have to correct *my* bad habits
because of my bad conditioning, if you want to put it that
way, so that I can respond openly to him. It's worked with
me, personally. Now, with Americans, I have to revert back
to the old way. Therefore you live sort of a schizophrenic
life over here. But it's not as bad as in America. I mean
you go out here and speak to the average Frenchman and
he can be rude to you and if you don't know the Parisian
mentality you might say, "It's because I'm black" or "because I'm American," but he'll turn around and the guy
behind you will be French and he'll treat him the same
way. So you get a sort of equality. I think the Parisians are
rude, but they're rude to everybody—they just don't single
anybody out.

Q: *What is your feeling when a white American ap-
proaches you over here?*

Well, it's according to what kind of white American you're talking about. My first reaction is that my guard goes up—my sixth sense or whatever you want to call it comes back into play again. I have been here long enough that I will extend friendliness, but I will watch his attitude toward me very carefully.

Q: *How about the black American abroad? What happens when you run into him?*

Well, it's "somebody from home." Again, it comes down to the fact that we speak the same language, we have a certain rapport. And so the gates open. Later you might discover this is a mistake or the guy might be a slob but at first the gates open immediately.

Q: *Have you run into American Negroes who avoid other American Negroes?*

Oh, yes. It happened to me in Spain—Barcelona. There was a Negro couple—they were a little older than I was— walking down the street and you know I went up and spoke to them and they almost jumped off the pavement and ran. I've seen that, too. When I was working for the *Tribune,* I saw it a couple of times. I ran into a couple of Negro chicks walking around Paris, attractive girls, and of course I spoke to them but they wouldn't speak. Again, it's a matter of personality. Maybe they thought I should not have been flirting with them.

But I have learned one thing about all Americans, black or white: in a foreign country their first attitude is fear. When a situation arises, friendly or unfriendly, there is a language barrier, and the first attitude toward that is fear. I learned this in the five years I've been here. You approach somebody on the street or they approach you, you recognize them as American and there's fear right away. I'll give you a case in point. I met a white American and, I assume, his wife, looking for a street. I speak a little French and as I walked by I saw a problem there, so I offered my services. Right away, there was fear! They thought I was out to take them, probably, to pull the Murphy game. Whereas, to turn that around, if *I* was in Austria or any of these countries and I walked up to somebody and said, "Look, I'm lost," in whatever language I could communicate in, the attitude would be to help me, without worrying about it. And I have *yet* to be taken by the Murphy game.

Another classic example—I was in Austria and I was trying to find a youth hostel. I had a motor scooter, a Lambretta. There was an old woman on the street and I asked her if she could tell me where the hostel was, and she walked five blocks out of her way to show it to me. Now, if I had approached an American and done that, they would have been afraid—"Who's this, what does he want?"

Q: *Do you feel that white Americans behave differently over here?*

Oh, yes! They're much more polite, especially if they're talking to a black American. Less condescending. They don't get that tone in their voice. But again, you have to realize that there's a certain class of Americans who come over here and they are often more sophisticated, more tolerant. Now if you want to run into the kind you seem to meet all the time in the States, you'll find *them* mostly among the servicemen. But the tourists usually come from a different intellectual and economic level, and they tend to relax more.

Q: *Do you go to the American Express office here?*

No. Only about once every three months. That's the limit they'll hold mail. And that's just in case someone is trying to send me a letter that way. I very rarely go down there. In fact, I rarely go on the Right Bank except on business.

Q: *How much do the black people here think about the civil rights movement and to what extent do they identify with it?*

Well, I'm going to speak for me. I read the newspapers every day. I try to keep track as best I can of what's going on.

Q: *Are there any civil rights organizations here?*

I just read here in the paper that they have an office of SNCC, the Student Non-Violent Coordinating Committee here.

Q: *Have you ever come into contact with any other kind of organizations here involving American Negroes, that has civil rights as its concern?*

Well, I was involved in a movement to try and get Malcolm X to come here and speak for the second time, after he was refused entry, and our object was strictly to have him come here and speak on Afro-American problems. There is also this organization here called PARIS. It's an abbreviation for something, a racial integration society or something of that nature. They are associated with SNCC here.

Q: *Do you have any feelings about not being in the States at this particular time?*

None at all. Because I feel this way: I am an American black man and I always will be. That's where my roots are. I couldn't possibly consider myself French or whatever country I happen to live in, you know, but I don't feel any longing to go back because I'm missing the struggle or anything like that. Because to me, the struggle is worldwide. It's the haves versus the have-nots. And the United States is but a small spoke in one whole large wheel. That struggle is happening in Asia, and in Latin America. It's also happening in Africa. The haves against the have-nots, or the class struggle, if you want to call it that.

Q: *So that no matter where you are, you're involved.*

Exactly. The fact that I carry my skin with me means I have to have opinions—about the French or the Italians or anybody else.

Q: *You said earlier that you're aware there is a certain kind of prejudice here—have you any personal evidence of this?*

The only personal example I've had so far happened when I was on the Métro once about two years ago with a girl. Some fellow who spoke French fluently and very quickly began "loud-talking" me—I didn't understand what he was talking about, for he suddenly began talking out of the clear blue sky, with no reason. I hadn't antagonized him in any way. I was preoccupied with this girl I was escorting. The only thing I did understand were the words *pauvre fille* which means "poor girl," but I was angry and that also stops me from speaking French the way I might want to. I didn't understand all of what he said but the context and the tone of his voice was obvious. That's the only personal thing that's happened to me in the five years I've been here.

Q: *How about things like getting an apartment?*

Well, one of my friends has a whole repertoire about this but I, personally, have had no trouble. Not if I've got the money to spend. It comes down to the economics of "Can I afford the rent?" Now, I may have been refused on grounds of color on certain occasions but, if I have, the French were very good at hiding the fact that their refusal was a racial thing. I've also noticed, in talking to a few French people in my courtyard here, that I am seen as an American *mestizo,* a mulatto. That, to them, is different from being an African. I don't see it but they do. That's it. I'm a *mulatte.* In all of Europe, I'm a *mulatte.*

Q: *Do you have any feelings about penetrating the society here—do you feel as though you can?*

I've been here five years and I can matter-of-factly say

that I have been invited into French families' homes to socialize just two times—just twice. Parisians—at certain levels, of course—are very cold people. In my opinion they take their whole life very seriously and they just don't seem to want to trade social calls—you know, the way we do at home. To a Frenchman, your home is your castle and you keep the outside world out. There's not much socializing *at home*.

Q: *Do you feel that as a lack?*

No. There is one thing I must say. I don't really like Paris. If I could move, I would go to a climate where it's warm with mountains and sea. I don't like cold weather although I grew up in Detroit. After three years of living in California, I got sort of used to sunshine and I like that. The only reason I don't go back to California is that it happens to be in the United States. I would like to go back for a visit, though. And I do miss the sea.

I like the fact that I'm left alone here. I live in the courtyard and everybody here knows I'm American and that I come and go and that I'm an artist. That gives me a certain liberty. I can sleep to eleven o'clock and they don't think anything about it. Or come in at four in the morning and they don't think anything of that. They leave my private life alone and I like that. I think that's characteristic of Parisians.

In American society, I feel, what you think *is* important, people like to know what you think. They are not so interested in what you *do,* it's what you think about whatever is going on. That's one of the things I don't like about my country. In France, you can talk to a business associate about his mistresses and he'll talk to you all you want about that. But don't talk about his politics because that's his personal business and you don't discuss that. And you don't talk about his business affairs. In the States it's the

other way around: Your business and your financial life
are open to public scrutiny as are your politics, but your
personal life is real tight. What it comes down to here is
that they leave the individual alone. Some people don't
like that, they like that camaraderie, the neighborly thing.
I happen to know *my* neighbor because he's an American
and he lives next door. But the people downstairs I know
very little except to say hello and good-by to.

Q: *Do you feel a great lack of tension about race here?*

Oh, yes. The tension is in my house because I happen to
be a black American. I read the newspapers, I get upset. I
don't like what goes on in Watts, in Selma. I don't like
what goes on over there, period. But I walk out in the
street here and it's not there. I was told something by an
Afro-American friend of mine, a writer who used to live
here. He pointed out something about the black children's
faces here—there's no strain in them, no sign of tension.
Now, all right, the French, they're white and they have
their views and by some standards they are prejudiced but
it doesn't seem to affect the whole bonemarrow of the society like it does over there. You see children of all colors
racing up and down the streets and nobody worries about
it. A classic example: You see a white mother walking
down the street pushing a buggy. She has one black child
in the buggy and three black children walking with her.
People don't turn around. They just walk past. If a black
child runs into the corner store, the owner says, *"Bon jour,
petit chou,"* like he says to all the rest of the children, from
what I've seen.

Q: *Is there a reaction when you and your Swedish wife,
Kerstin, walk down the street together here?*

Of course there is, she's an attractive woman. So men
stare but it's not the same hostile stare you get from Americans which she has seen here, and which she had not seen

before. It's wonderful seeing Americans—she hasn't been to the States yet—through her eyes. Because she comes up with all these questions I don't think of any more. I've been away from it so long.

For example, my attitude toward women working. I don't want her to work because right now she would support me. I don't want that. American women seem to think there's something wrong with her because she doesn't want to work—American men also. But you see, I don't want that.

I've learned this: if a man has a dream that he wants to accomplish and he has a European woman, she'll accept that dream. At home, a lot of them say, "That's all well and good, but what about the bacon?" It comes down to that, you see. Now, I have a dream. I want to do something. It's important to me and also to the stability of this house that I do it my way, and on my terms. Well, now, I happen to have a woman who digs that. To put it simply. If I had an American woman, I doubt that she would. Of course there's always a chance, but I doubt it.

After all, it's been touch and go for a year for us. There have been times when we've lacked money for rent and food, the very basics. But the only complaint I get from her is about cigarettes, that's the only thing she really wants.

I've been criticized about her not working by Afro-Americans as well as white Americans. But I have yet to be criticized on this by a European man or woman.

Now, I'm not saying European women don't want security, but I have been watching the other fellows and their European girl friends and I think if they have something they want to accomplish the girl will go along with it.

Q: *Let's go back to the beginning, about your leaving the U.S.*

I didn't run away, no. I didn't leave there with the idea

that I had to find another, better place to live. I didn't develop that frame of mind till I was over here for a while. Then I began to look around and to analyze, and to compare things, that I remembered from home, with what was happening here. Then I decided that a man shouldn't have to live like that anywhere in the world. I'm not saying this is Utopia here. I'm not even looking for Utopia, for me that would be boring. But we're talking about matters of degree.

Q: *What about the Algerians? The way they are treated here, how do you feel about that?*

My personal opinion is that they are the Afro-Americans or the Negroes of France. But they have one important advantage. They can go home where they aren't different! A Frenchman, with whom I was discussing Algerians, once told me, "They're not Christians! They're different. They treat their women differently. They don't have the same mentality." And while he was saying all this, I could hear Senator Eastland or somebody like that saying the very same thing about *me*. This happened in sixty or sixty-one and it was my first exposure to that. I said to myself, *"This is new!"* The Frenchman was talking to *me* as an equal but yet he was talking about the Algerian as a subperson, someone below him.

Q: *How did that make you feel?*

Well, I told him that that's how they felt about *us* at home. He said, "Well, I don't understand that." He said, "Because you're just as educated and you're just as cultured," and on and on. Now, I'm completely different in his mind from the Algerian. So this prejudice thing gets to be a funny, interweaving paradox, you understand. There has been a great influx here of Senegalese and others from French Africa. They seem to be mostly performing menial jobs.

To the French, I'm an American. *Un noir.* They see us

with Cadillacs on television programs from America. Then there's the average American Negro in the ghetto in Watts. That man lives better than his counterpart here in France, materially speaking. So they can't understand the actual problem. They can look down on the African, it seems, because the French still run French Africa.

Q: *Do they know about the level of material achievement of some Negroes in America?*

Oh yes, indeed. You better believe that. Remember, now that we have Telstar, it's on television all the time. They see the American black man and his house, five or six rooms, whereas the average person at the same level in Paris here, the Frenchman, lives in two. A guy in Watts may have his Cadillac or Jaguar even though he got it on the credit system, while the French guy is lucky to get a *Deux Cheveaux* or to have a car at all. Parisians are very conscious of material wealth. To us Americans, a refrigerator, a gas range, a car, these are ordinary things you can have and still be poor.

Q: *Do you miss not being able to be in politics here?*

Oh, of course. And I care about politics. But I happen to be an artist and it's hard to be that and be actively involved in politics. I feel the two don't mix. To be politically active is a full-time job. If you're an artist, that's a lifetime career. But I try to keep aware of what's going on.

Q: *Have you made up your mind definitely to stay out of the U.S.?*

I'm thinking about it and I've been thinking about it a long time now. Kerstin will tell you that I can be homesick for San Francisco. I talk about it a lot, especially when the weather here gets bad. In the summer, as you know, the weather here can be awful.

And so, after five years absence and reading about the

changes in America, I would sort of like to go back and see what it looks like. *As a tourist!* Meaning I will definitely have my round-trip ticket before I leave here so if I decide I don't want to stay, I can just leave.

Q: *Have you thought about trying to become a French citizen?*

Well, as I said, I don't like Paris. I'm not in love with France, or the French culture, or even the French language. I do love French cooking. But cooking is not a reason to take on citizenship of a country. I happen to be American, I think as an American, I carry an American passport and I feel like an American. I can't pass for anything else. The French see me and immediately think I'm an American or I'm from Martinique. The way I dress, the clothes and everything else show me as an American. I don't try to change my habits. I happen to be a citizen of the United States and I am not going to systematically go and destroy that. But I also know that I can with a U.S. passport live anywhere in the world I want to, outside of the Iron Curtain countries. There are 110 countries in the world today and I may find a place which I might want to call home. And when I call it home, that doesn't mean I'm going to say, "All right, America, here's your passport back." I look at a passport as a tool to get me across borders, period.

Q: *Prejudice in the U.S. stems frequently from male sexual jealousy on the part of whites and the male usually determines the tone of the society. Does the Frenchman see the Negro as a sexual rival?*

I don't think so. Because he has his own ego. He would never be caught dead admitting that somebody else—any man, not just the black man—is sexually his superior. Because when it comes to man-woman relationships in Paris it is, to my knowledge, a personal thing. If you can't hold your woman, that's *your* personal problem and has nothing to do with race. Or the size of the genitals or what not. Now, in the States, they do have a definite sexual hang-up. That conditioning comes in again. The French male might not like a specific interracial situation but his dislike will have nothing to do with any preconditioning.

Let a Negro girl come here and if she's attractive, watch the line form behind her! I will say one thing I've noticed about Europeans in general: black people, American or otherwise, are considered particularly attractive here. Let's leave England and Germany aside—I feel, based on what I've seen while traveling through Europe, that Europeans, with the exception of the English and the Germans, find black people attractive. And I also think whites feel the same thing *in the States*, which is why all those sexual laws were introduced there. The difference is that there they don't want to *admit* it. When I was in Rome I met an Afro-American girl who was, frankly, not attractive. She was big, she was fat. I don't know what your taste in women is, but according to mine she was not attractive. But the Italian men *loved* her! The point is, here was a girl hitchhiking, and the only thing she had to do was put her bags out on the highway then sit in the roadside café and a traffic jam would happen! She had something in the neighborhood of eleven proposals of marriage, some man put her up in his villa, without any sexual attempt (so she says) and when we walked down the street women stared in pure envy, men completely "lost their cool."

Q: *At least one newspaper in Paris has written sympathetically of Britain's racial problems and posed the old chestnut, "What would be your reaction to a black man marrying your sister or daughter?" assuming, I think, that many French would object. Would they?*

I would say that they do, basically. But it's according to

the kind of family. Perhaps in a middle-class family they would. But I have seen another reaction, also. On the Champs Élysées, where I was selling my newspapers, I walked into the big café, Fouquet's. A Rolls-Royce drives up and this very chic French couple get out, obviously wealthy, and with this child who is as black as black can get. It must have been their grandson or adopted child. There he was, and he was as much a part of that French family as he could be. And I said to myself, "Now that's nice, isn't it?" I had never seen *that* in the States. And there was no attention paid to them except by the few Americans who were there. Whoever else looked at them, did so because of the obvious wealth—I watched that carefully—and I thought, "Because I'm an American *I'm* watching them," but the French are paying no attention to it at all.

Charles H. Nichols:

BERLIN

What does a black man do when he decides to leave America? Does he look around for an ideal society, some bigot-proof Utopia where he may finally disconnect his color-sensitive ganglia, turn off his Jim Crow Early Warning System? The evidence suggests not. For the black expatriate, the country of his residence may be chosen for any one of a number of very practical reasons: a place where he can ply his particular skills, an immigration system or a labor union that is at least willing to give him a chance to make a go of it, a society that has not constructed institutions that depend upon his permanent subjection. He knows he may still encounter instances of bias in any European country, particularly in nations in which American troops have ever spent any time.

Germany, of course, did not need the Americans to stir up ethnocentric passions. Under the Nazis it had its own racial dogmas and a category of officially designated lesser folk, among them the Negro. But to a number of U.S. Negroes, Germany today is seen as a country where pigmentation is not something that arouses antipathies or anxieties. In opera, black singers perform in roles that might be deemed unsuitable for a Negro in America, and in Berlin, Munich and Hamburg, black musicians are venerated as the only authentic purveyors of jazz.

Charles H. Nichols is a small man with a large head, horn-rimmed glasses and an aura of self-assurance. He teaches American literature at the John F. Kennedy Institute for American Studies at the Free University of Berlin. On his way to his book-lined office, he can see the green uniforms of American Army personnel streaming in and out of a nearby U.S. military installation on Clay Allee. To Professor Nichols, it is a daily reminder of a world he left behind . . . almost.

Charles H. Nichols

I was born in Brooklyn, New York. I went to Boys' High School in Brooklyn, and Brooklyn College. Then Brown University in Providence where I earned my Ph. D. in English in 1948. I taught for many years at Hampton Institute in Virginia, at Morgan State College in Baltimore—both, as you know, are Negro institutions. I also taught elsewhere as a guest professor.

In 1954 I was a Fulbright Professor at Aarhus University in Denmark and that was my first trip abroad.

It was on that trip that I was offered a lecture tour through Germany and I did that. One of the universities I visited then was the one I am now connected with, the

Free University of Berlin. When I was teaching at Hampton, it struck me increasingly that there was really no point to living in a part of the world where you're surrounded by hostile people. Why should I continue to live in the South?

Virginia, of course, was not a totally unpleasant place, and Hampton Institute is a very pleasant place to live if you don't mind a rather confined situation. At the time I was there a black person couldn't even drink a coke down at the drugstore in the town of Hampton. I was back there in 1961 and I was very glad to see that had been changed, and I was also very enthusiastic about the kind of effort the students were making in civil rights protests. Many things my colleagues and friends thought were sheer nonsense when I said them at Hampton some years before were now the common talk. I felt very happy about this.

But I think the intellectual confinement at Hampton was felt very keenly by most of the people who taught there. They had an interracial staff, actually a fairly good staff for a small college, but among the better students, of course, there was a very strong feeling of isolation, too. The more active students were always attempting to create a situation in which they would be more challenged, in which they would have more outlets to express themselves. And although most of the college administrations at Hampton have been rather conservative and fearful, in the last years I think they are somewhat more—well, of course, things have changed—they are somewhat more liberal and intelligent on these matters than they were.

My older boy is now almost fourteen and the younger is eleven. The older one goes to a German gymnasium, which is sort of like a high school, although it's somewhat more advanced. He has all of his instructions in German and he does very well, actually. The other one is in a school which was established some years ago, a cooperative school organized for German and foreign children. Most of the foreigners there are American.

I think the thing that impressed me most on my first visit to Europe was the phenomenon of Europe itself. I think that an American is drawn to Europe basically because so much of his education consists of orientation in European culture, in European history. I think one has the feeling he's getting to the source when one gets to Europe. When I got here I thought: "Imagine—there's all this here that I haven't seen before!" The experience of being here for a year the first time was, for me, like another college education. There was a whole vast range of experiences that struck me very forcibly. One of them was the phenomenon of art in the lives of the people of Europe. The United States is a very large, dynamic, pluralistic and interesting country in many ways, but artistically it's primitive.

For instance, when we came from New York, we landed in Oslo. And we took a little tour of the town. We went to Frogner Park where they have those enormous statues of the human family, large naked statues of men and women in various aspects of love-making. This kind of thing in a public park! It's a fantastic thing for an American to see for the first time. He thinks, "My God, the League of Decency would never permit this at home." Or take Rome and Florence where all the walls and ceilings and floors of the buildings are decorated so beautifully. So much to feed the eye. This is, for me, a fantastic thing.

We ran through the Louvre—it was ridiculous, of course, just to spend a day in the Louvre—but we had only six days in Paris. So we spent the day trotting through the Louvre, of course, not seeing half of it. Or going through the Vatican Museum. It was just overwhelming.

This, I think, for me, was the most powerful impact: the sense of generations of culture, none of it devoted to commercial use or profit, but merely to this—a kind of enlargement of the spirit. I thought this was great, and it is one of the things that I must say I liked about Europe. Another thing I liked is the mature outlook Europeans have on matters such as sex, and communism. These are not the bogymen they are for Americans. In America you're constantly being hampered by fearful notions about sex and by people who say that you shouldn't teach Lincoln Steffens' autobiography to high school children and things like that. You don't encounter that sort of thing much here. Although there *is* a puritanical movement now in Germany called *Saubere Leinwand*. It literally means "the clean screen," the screen on which one projects motion pictures, or the television screen. But this movement is small—this attempt to keep sex from being too frankly portrayed on television, in the cinema and mass media. I don't think anybody here takes this very seriously.

I have lived in four or five different houses here in Berlin. In things like renting houses, professors come first here. Not one agent or owner has hesitated or even looked as if he might, and I now live in a section which is sort of like Westchester back in New York. I could not live with those kinds of people anywhere in America. In the first place I couldn't afford it, and in the second place, they simply wouldn't have me. It is a great support to one's ego when you feel you don't have to fight the business of race all the time, and can feel that whatever you have achieved in your profession counts for something.

In America, on the other hand, I had the feeling throughout my career that though I was a bright little boy in school, did my work in college, got my degrees, published my articles and went to all my professional meetings, I knew they weren't going to give me the call to Harvard in any damn case. You know what I mean? I must say that I was, and still am, somewhat bitter about the kind of experiences I had in my attempts to get a job as a college teacher commensurate with my abilities, outside the Negro college circuit. I talked to various people, one of them the chairman at one New York college—I was interested in applying there in about 1957. He was an extremely condescending man who took the attitude, "Well, you know, you've achieved a great deal *for a Negro*." He never for a moment entertained the idea of hiring me. Others took another line: "Well, actually you're a person who's had the sort of experience in publishing and so on to whom we could only offer a senior post." So they wouldn't offer me what I could easily have taken. And they certainly weren't going to offer me a full professorship. I didn't even expect that. But it was unmistakably a kind of discrimination. They should have offered me these things and then let *me* decide whether I wanted them or not.

I feel very much involved in what's going on in civil rights in America. Very much concerned and very eager to see progress. I'm also happy about the progress that has been made. But underlying all of this I have a persistent feeling of bitterness that Negroes should have had to go to these extremes to call these questions to everyone's attention, and I have to keep warning European audiences, when they read about the passing of the Civil Rights Act or the speeches of President Johnson, that the situation of the average little Negro in Los Angeles or someplace in Alabama is not very different from what it ever was. And that all these things will have, of course, their slow working, but that the kind of fundamental economic and political changes which are needed in America are still not coming. Even the "war on poverty" is more like a pop gun than a war.

I encounter a large number of American guest professors who show something of their surprise at finding me here, and they frequently ask me, "How come you're a regularly appointed professor at a university here?" But the thing that strikes me about them, to get back to the problem, is the way in which some of them have made the attempt over here, in discussing the racial situation in America, to make it appear as if that situation is really much better than it appears in German newspapers, that "you mustn't think that the situation is bad."

In 1962, for example, we had a professor from San Diego, California, who insisted that Negroes were by and large satisfied, that they were making so much progress that the Negro was as free, virtually, as anyone else. In a talk afterward, I said I thought this was a great oversimplification of the question and that *I* was sure that the situation in the United States would soon come to a virtual explosion. This turned out to be an amazing prophecy, because immediately afterward we had Birmingham and then later Watts in Los Angeles.

I feel I've devoted perhaps twenty years of my life to teaching in the South, to writing and polemics, and discussions, and God knows what, to protest on the Negro question. So I don't feel guilty about not being there now. On the contrary, I feel that I probably serve better where I am. Because the problem is a world problem. Then there's one's self . . . you're no good to anyone unless you're fulfilling your own needs.

I think it's very likely that I had reached a point of diminishing returns. I don't know if you know the Negro colleges well, but Hampton is a much better one than most. Still a Negro college is a very frustrating place to be, in many ways. The thing I miss from Hampton was the pleasant, informal, warm, friendly human relations that one had with students and all the members of the faculty. A European university is a much more impersonal place. But on the other hand I don't think that a Negro college *really* provides what a student *or* a teacher needs. I think that the very fact of segregation itself, even if the conditions are optimum, is a very great depressant on all forms of originality, creativity and intellectual activity.

One of the most crippling aspects of segregation is the way it limits one's cultural and intellectual horizons. I spent a lot of my time as a scholar, writing and researching on the Negro, and though in one way I don't really regret this, in a way I *do* resent it because I feel that this, too, is a kind of segregation, knowing that white audiences would not want to listen to you lecture on some other subject.

I would say that I consider my own experiences as a Negro in the United States by and large to be somewhat better than average. I grew up with white children in school and went to college with them. I still have a great many white friends to whom I feel very close and with whom I have never felt the usual unconsciously conde scending attitudes. That condescension was something I experienced in America frequently, even among educated people. When I encounter Europeans I have a great feeling of liberation in this respect. I don't mean to say that there is no racial prejudice in Europe and certainly in Germany with its past and its racial dogmas. But *my* experience has been rather positive. From the very beginning, the philosophical faculty in this university was rather proud of the fact that they had invited a Negro. Yet they didn't overdo it. They didn't behave as if this was some sort of great special gesture.

The ability to speak to people here in German allows

you, especially in smaller groups, to probe the attitudes of the individuals more closely and discover what layers of prejudice he may be concealing. On one occasion, I was asked to join other colored people, including the son of an African leader, an Indonesian minister who was in Berlin, and an Indian girl from New Delhi, in a discussion about color, the color problem amongst students, and the various adjustments which the foreign students must make in adapting to life in Berlin. Most of these people pointed out that the colored students have more difficulty getting rooms than the others. We talked about some of the attitudes that arise. The Indonesian said, for example, on one occasion while he was walking in the street with another Indonesian, a fat German woman came along and said to him, "Are you two cannibals?" He looked her in the eye and said, "Yes, and we especially enjoy eating fat women!" That, of course, got a laugh but I think that this kind of thing is probably very, very rare. I never encountered anything of this nature in Germany; I've always met scrupulous politeness and concern.

Occasionally the Nazi era and Hitler's teachings about nonwhite peoples come up in the course of discussion. The Germans themselves will bring it up. What I have frequently done is relate the racial attitudes of Americans to racial attitudes held by so-called scientists like Mueller and Gobineau from whom Hitler and his cohorts got these ideas. Some of these racist ideas still linger in the minds of the students. For example, after a public meeting some students and I were having a drink together and a German boy said he was convinced that, from the point of view of nature, there wasn't supposed to be intermarriage. That if you married outside your race, you might have some sort of freak for a child. Of course we all leaped on him at this point and said, "Where did you learn your science?" and

"What sort of evidence can you present for such an idea as that?" These people were very apologetic, however, and when we attacked their ideas they were truly injured. One girl broke into tears, saying "How can you think I'm prejudiced?"

Racism is a European idea. I have frequently said to some people in Europe, "You know, when you talk about America, remember these are ideas which have been carried abroad by Europeans. Everywhere in the world, Europeans have used race as a means of dominance. In Africa, in South America, in Asia, and everywhere else, so don't be so surprised by the fruits of your own sowing."

Status makes a lot more difference here than it does in America. In German society a professor is an exalted personality and I find that I sometimes get a little weary of the rarefied atmosphere in which a professor is supposed to move. Almost anywhere I go where I am known, I am treated like a celebrity. I felt a little uncomfortable about the attention at first but I'm getting used to it. I realize that it is not me that they are honoring, but the ideal of learning.

Gloria Davy:

BERLIN

*I had an appointment with a popular Negro per-
former of the Deutsche Oper in West Berlin and we
agreed to meet for lunch at my hotel, the Kempinsky. As
we entered the dining room, I mentioned my reservation
and the headwaiter went into a prolonged and agitated
discussion with his staff over where to seat us. Since it was
an early hour and there were rows of empty tables in plain
sight, I began to feel a vague uneasiness.*

*Finally the headwaiter led us, with a dramatic flourish,
to a small, plush inner dining room where, it turned out,
celebrities are often seated when they dine there. The staff
had been excited because they recognized my operatic
friend and wanted to give her a table fit for such an
honored guest!*

*As we talked, she told me of another incident in which a
visiting Negro friend mistakenly interpreted a remark he'd
overheard to be a slur upon Negroes and gotten himself*

involved in an altercation with two startled German busi-nessmen who had been talking, unaware of his nearby presence. "I told him that he'd have to stop being so sensi-tive over here," she recalls, "because he was reacting without really knowing what these people were saying. He was so used to that kind of slur in the States that he still had his dukes up over here."

Apart from the problems they sometimes encounter in German cities with American bases, such as Frankfurt, most Negroes in the professions in that country manage to do well and gradually the preoccupations with color re-cede.

Another Deutsche Oper artist, Gloria Davy, confirms that for her, life in Germany has been rewarding. She is married to Hermann Peningfeld, a German businessman, and is the mother of a small son. The Peningfelds divide their year between their home in Berlin and another residence in Geneva, Switzerland.

Gloria Davy

There is a simple fact here that Europeans just accept: you are a different person, you are a Negro. In America, nobody wants to face that fact and this makes for much confusion . . . on both sides. They insist, "You're exactly like we are," when we are not really, I mean just from a purely physical point of view. Everybody sort of wants to skim over this truth and that complicates the matter so much. It would be much simpler if we really just started facing the down-to-earth facts.

People in Europe ask you questions because they want

to find out things about these differences. In America people are ashamed to do this perhaps because they have bad consciences or thoughts which are not good and so they are embarrassed to ask you an obvious question. Here they may ask you, "How do you like living in Europe?" "Have you adjusted well?" "Was it difficult to adjust?" or perhaps, "Is it very much different from the States?" People just ask these questions. That's a normal reaction.

I think people in the States have feelings that the social code forbids their expressing, that's the whole point I'm getting at. And so we don't start from the bottom, as two human beings. We try instead to build on a foundation which is really very shaky. We start with a whole set of false concepts and pretenses.

Actually, I didn't leave America for any racial reasons, for any reasons of dissatisfaction. I left America as one hundred of my white colleagues leave America—to come to Europe and find a place to sing, because there was no place to sing in America a few years ago. If you look on the list of every German opera house, three-quarters of the people are Americans. Here at the Deutsche Oper Berlin, there is not one performance where there are fewer than two or three leading singers who are American. Because we have almost no opera houses in America.

The Germans, on the other hand, have no singers. They got scattered during the war. The Italians have come out with a whole lot of singers but the Germans only have a few. They have, however, many more opera houses than other countries. There's an opera house in every middle village and they don't have the singers to fill them, so they're taking foreign singers. Actually some of the very best singers to be had are Americans. They're the best trained.

There's another point, and that is, there are not very many good voice teachers here. I would say most of them were probably Jewish or part Jewish and most are in New York now. There are many German voice teachers in America—as well as Hungarians, Czechoslovakians, Viennese.

I studied at the Juilliard School of Music in New York and my coming to Europe was sort of coincidental. I hadn't really planned it. I came over as Bess in *Porgy and Bess* in 1954. I replaced Leontyne Price, who had been with the company for two years, and I toured with the company for fourteen months. We sang at La Scala in Milan, and the people there became interested in me; they thought I had the makings of an opera singer.

They talked me into leaving the company to stay in Milan to study opera—because I was originally prepared as a concert singer—and that's what I did. I left the company and we sang at Scala in February and I stayed with the company until June when I went back to the States for two months. I wanted to get myself organized to come back. I returned in September and moved to Milan. I stayed for five years and my career—my European career—started in Italy, then spread throughout Europe.

There was nothing racial about the fact that I couldn't get a job in New York. After all, I left in 1954—and in 1958 I made my debut at the Metropolitan. So I made it when a lot of white colleagues didn't. No, in America the problem is lack of opera houses. Now there are many more than there used to be, say, ten years ago. Ten years ago there was only the Metropolitan in New York, one in San Francisco and one in Chicago. And that was that. And for those you had to be a finished product. But where could you get your training? That was the point. That's why everybody fled over here, because here you can go to any little village and get a contract in an opera house for two years and then you're "routine," a regular performer.

I had been in Europe prior to my coming over with *Porgy and Bess*. I was in Paris in 1952 for two weeks with Virgil Thomson's Opera, *Four Saints in Three Acts,* singing in the chorus. I had been studying at Juilliard and took that job at the Winter Garden at night. It was sort of a Broadway show but half opera, half musical. I think it played a month on Broadway and then we went to Paris. That was my first time in Europe.

I recall that trip very vividly. Paris is an overwhelming city. When I was there that first time, I was very young. I shared a room with two other chorus girls at a hotel. Olga James was one—we were at Juilliard together—and another girl, Doris Mayes. We just went wild, absolutely berserk. We had so much fun we never got to bed and it was a smashing two weeks.

I was born in New York but my parents are West Indian. I lived in Brooklyn, was born in Brooklyn, raised in Brooklyn. I went to the High School of Music and Art.

I do not feel my life in New York was at all difficult. As a matter of fact, it was marvelous. I've often said to my husband that I was a very big girl before I realized I was poor. I felt no great racial pressure—none whatsoever. When I lived in Brooklyn, a Bedford-Stuyvesant section didn't exist, and I remember quite distinctly that my playmates were Italian or Jewish; there were not many Negro families in Brooklyn then. When I went to school in Brooklyn it was the same. I have no idea what it's like now. At the High School of Music and Art it was ninety-five per cent white. It was and is a highly specialized school; you have to take an admissions examination, a musical examination and an intelligence examination. You have to have a certain IQ besides being musically talented. I remember that, when I was accepted, the people at my elementary school, P.S. 129, were so proud of me because I was the first person from that school to be admitted to the High School of Music and Art. Many people had tried and I was the first to be accepted, and it was a grand thing. At that time, Music and Art was not quite ten years old and, as I said, had but a handful of Negroes. I think that was probably because not that many people knew about the school. *I* hadn't known about it. But fortunately at P.S. 129 there was a music teacher who thought I was a special talent, and when it came time for me to choose a high school she was the one who suggested to my mother that I try for Music and Art. We had never heard of it. Otherwise, I would have gone to any other academic high school.

So there was no pressure in my life at all that I can think of. As a matter of fact, I think almost everything I have accomplished is due to my days at Music and Art. This gave me a foundation, musically, intellectually, socially, and at the proper age. The age of twelve, you know, at which impressions are so lasting. I think this had a great deal to do with the kind of person and the kind of artist I am today.

Over here I lived in Milan five years until I married in 1959. My husband is Hermann Peningfeld, a business-man.

My mother was with me when I was in *Porgy and Bess* and she was traveling around with me for three or four months. When we went for a walk, by the time we'd gone half a block we had a crowd of people following us, just looking and saying, "Oh, how beautiful . . . *che bella!*" It was nerve-racking, I can tell you. Now it's much different. I mean, they still look, but before you couldn't really move along anywhere.

I didn't know any Italian when I came here, just *"buon giorno"* and *"buona sera."* But I learned it rather quickly. I had to, because I was completely alone, and also because my Italian voice teacher spoke very little English. I had an Italian manager who spoke English but refused to speak it with me, and an Italian maid who spoke no English, so in four months I was speaking Italian. When you have to, you'd be amazed at how quickly you learn, and it's an easy language, too. Italians are very patient with people who are trying to learn their language. They love to have foreigners speak Italian. That's in contrast to the French, who put you down. The Italians keep patting you on the back and telling you how wonderfully you're doing and you really learn. It's such a beautiful language anyway.

It's always been harder to penetrate French society. France is like this for any foreigner. You will hardly ever find foreigners setting foot in French homes. We lived in Geneva and Geneva is very French since it's just on the French border of Switzerland, and it's the same way there. They will invite you three times a week to a restaurant for dinner but never to their homes. It's a very peculiar thing. The Swiss-Germans are completely different.

Paris is not so bad, but if you go into the provinces of France, they probably don't even talk to you. Not out of any animosity or hostility, they're just a closed society.

In Italy they are just the opposite. If you go there as an architect or an engineer or anything else, they will accept you, absolutely. There are classes in Italy, of course, and they stick very much to their class. Milan, for example, abounds in upper classes—it is a very wealthy city—and they're sort of closed. But the exclusiveness is not based on money, it's based on fame, intellect or background. I get on well in Milan. I still have many friends there, wonderful friends.

Rome is completely different. I've spent a lot of time there but I've never lived there. It's a sort of wild, free city like Paris, but in an Italian way. It's much more bohemian. I would also say it's much less serious, but it's a beautiful city and we had a wonderful time. It is, however, full of foreigners.

We've had our present house here in Berlin for one year. Before that I had a small apartment not far from here, around the corner, also for one year. I decided it would be a good idea if I had one place where I was more or less permanent, so that I would not be so much away from my son in his early years. I signed a three-year contract with the opera house for forty performances a year within six months—so that for at least six months of the year he would be by my side.

I'm not actually a resident member here, because I couldn't sign a contract for a long, long time, and a resident member is required to be here twelve months of the year—with a six weeks' vacation.

My status here is very peculiar. I'm sort of a permanent guest. Most of the other singers are here twelve months of the year, and when they want to go somewhere else they have to have a release from this opera house.

The opera here and all over Germany goes on all year except for six weeks during the summer. So you see, there are really opportunities to sing. Especially when you think of our four little opera houses in America, of which the Metropolitan has the longest season, and that is only October until April. San Francisco has something like eight weeks, as does Chicago.

I used to go back to America at the rate of three times a

year for singing engagements. The frequency of my visits has dwindled since I've had the baby, but I go at least once a year. I'll go next year, probably. I still have a family there, two sisters, a brother, and my father. I still see my friends when I go back. Most of them don't understand why I don't return to the States. They find it very strange that I can manage to live away from America. They keep saying, "But when are you going to come home?" But that is no longer home to me. Now I have a European husband, I have a half-European child—his mother is an American but *he* was born in Europe—how can I call America home? Actually, *my* family is now *here*. But my friends there don't quite understand this. They still think "one of these days she's going to come with her knapsack on her back and settle down." But they're wrong, Europe is absolutely home for me.

I still have my American citizenship. I don't see any reason for giving it up. It's just that simple. Our son has a German passport. He's German, because in Europe you are what your father is. However, he also has an American passport because I am an American.

I've often been asked if coming to Europe didn't give me a sense of freedom. But I didn't come here for reasons of race. On the contrary, for a long time I felt oppressed *here* because I was something "special" which I was not used to being. There are some people who like that, people who love to be the center of attraction, to be stared at as if they were something in the zoo, but I am not one of them. This attention disturbed me greatly for many years.

In Italy the reason for the staring was one hundred per cent positive. They thought I was a raving beauty, and this was also very alarming—I'd never heard this before. I don't like it. I love to be the center of attraction when I'm on the stage, that's my job, and that's where I want to show my best, but when I'm off it I want to be one of the crowd. And this was not possible.

Now it's much better. First of all, there are many more colored people here now. There are Indians and Chinese and others, but at *that* time I think there were literally three colored people in the whole of Milan.

There have been one or two remarks made to me by people, Americans, about the fact that I'm here sort of passively sitting it out while Negroes fight for their freedom in America, but I didn't run over here last year when everything started or the year before. I've been here now eleven years. I feel that as a woman my first duty is to my son and my husband. I can't just pack up my bags and say, "You two sit still, I'm going over to America and fight for civil rights!" even apart from the fact that I have a career to maintain here. I'm just not that patriotic. I want to see the person who is.

Is there anything like a "typical" reaction when I encounter a white American? Well, the white American abroad is much different from the white American at home. Here he wants to show the whole of Europe how democratic he is, you know, and he's pumping your hand five or six hundred times in a row, and patting you on the back and calling you by your first name and oh, he's "so happy" and "we should have dinner together," and everything, but when he gets home I want to see how fast he's going to invite you to an exclusive East Side restaurant. But over here they're very generous, extremely generous.

Of course to talk about "whites in general" is like talking about "Negroes in general"—they don't exist, you know. I have many white friends in New York—the best white friends I have in New York are mostly European Jews. And then to a person in the arts—you consider yourself an artist and he's an artist and she's an artist and you really don't look about to see who's colored and who's white. You're considering who's better and who's worse and who's got the most talent; you really don't worry about color or race.

What I miss most when I return to America I would say, generally, is *courtesy*. Just the general act of good behavior from one person to the next person, a certain standard of manners which is not to be found in America. Taxi drivers in America are impossible. Bus drivers are even worse, wherever you go. But Germany is becoming the same way—almost. They're following in America's footsteps. As countries become more and more industrialized this sort of creeps in. But it doesn't change the Italians—luckily. They work harder now, but they don't lose their manners. Maybe they don't go home for a lunch that takes three hours, but they go home for an hour and a half. Nobody's going to make them change that and they are perfectly right. I am with them one hundred per cent! I don't think anybody can change the Italians. That's probably why I love them so.

There *are* things about America that I don't find here— lots of things. Just start with food, and then go on. I was just in America in June and it hit me very strongly that there are some wonderful things in America which they don't have here. But those things are all on a certain superficial level—like bargain sales. It's very funny. These are trivial things for an American but when you haven't had them in a long time, you really start to appreciate them. You go into department stores in the U.S. and there are wonderful but reasonable things like bed linen and towels and these "dollar sales." Things like that don't exist over here. I didn't think about them for a long time, but when you see them again, you realize that this *is* something.

I do get a craving for certain food quite often. You can generally find almost everything—there are some special stores that cost an arm and a leg but they sell these American things, like cranberry sauce, sweet potatoes.

The first time I went back to the States after two years in Italy, I went back on the ship, *Cristoforo Colombo* and they had a buffet every night at midnight with roast turkey and cranberry sauce. I used to stay up every night, just for the turkey. I couldn't get enough turkey! One Thanksgiving I wandered all over Milan with another American girl and found a turkey, but we didn't have any cranberry sauce. We didn't have sweet potatoes either. But that buffet on the ship was really a feast.

Do you know Leroy Haynes' restaurant in Paris? When we were there with *Porgy and Bess* I tell you we used to run to that place—you can imagine, this whole Negro company—we flooded it. He never did such business in his life. And the cooking was so good! When we left he was very sweet and came to the train with his wife and one of the waiters and they brought boxes and boxes and boxes of fried chicken. I tell you, we were so happy.

Dean Dixon:

FRANKFURT

As is noted occasionally by some of the people in this book, a Negro can grow up in a ghetto in America where the inequities are so all-pervasive as to become an integral part of one's environment like the air we breathe or the weather we experience. One ceases to notice or wonder about them because they have always been there. In my childhood, a white adult acquaintance who was very interested in golf asked me why there were no outstanding professional golfers. Since I hadn't the slightest interest in golf and knew nothing of the color bar which existed then in that sport, I could not answer his question. At that time I would also probably have been at a loss to tell him why no Negro held the quarterback position in either of the professional football leagues despite the fact that Negroes have been prominent in pro football for decades. Yet the essential factor governing the absence of Negro quarter-

backs is the same as that which kept professional golf lily-white for years: color prejudice. Club owners were—and are—reluctant to put a black player in a spot where he would manage white players. (Admittedly coaches at the big white universities make this easier for the pros by rarely putting a Negro in collegiate quarterback positions, but since pro scouts have found some of the game's best players at all-Negro colleges, one wonders that quarter-backs have never been among them.)

Though the arts are widely assumed to present far more opportunities for the Negro, there is at least one area which has proved almost impenetrable: conducting. Yet there are American Negroes who conduct orchestras in Europe. The most prominent of these is 51-year-old Dean Dixon. Today Dixon is not only conductor of the Frankfurt Radio Orchestra, but also spends part of each year in Australia where he is conductor of the Sydney Symphony Orchestra. Dixon has conducted widely in Europe and has led the Sydney orchestra in a command performance for Queen Elizabeth II. He lives with his second wife, a Finnish noblewoman, and their children on a quiet, tree-lined street behind the American Consulate in Frankfurt.

Dean Dixon

I happened to be born in New York. My father was from Jamaica and my mother was from Barbados. They didn't get their American passport until about twenty to twenty-five years later. They weren't American citizens yet. So actually there is a lot of legal questioning as to whether I am an American or whether I only have an

American passport. Both my parents were Commonwealth citizens when I was born.

I really don't know. I never went into it. I didn't see their passports. I had nothing to do with passports until the first time I wanted to come to Europe, in forty-nine. I didn't need anything before that except a driver's license, which I had.

Q: *How about music—how did you get involved?*

When I was three and a half I made the mistake of walking around the dining room table with two sticks which my mother swears were in a violin position, and that was it. The next week the violin came into the house, a full-sized violin as big as I was and I couldn't hold it under my chin with both hands!

Q: *Were either of your parents involved in music?*

Not at all. But I developed asthma at a very early age and on bad-weather days I used to practice. Many times I was quite healthy and went out in the New York slush and snow and sat in school all day with wet shoes, then came home wheezing that night and was put to bed for a week or at least two or three days.

Q: *What was life like then, economically? More difficult than most or about average?*

More difficult than most. Partly because my parents were West Indian. My father had been trained as a lawyer but, when he came to America, that was a joke. He got himself a hotel job, a call boy in a hotel, and his salary was something like seven dollars every two weeks. They lived on what they were given for giving extra service. It was very up and down.

Q: *Where did you get your training as a child?*

First, Catholic school until the age of nine, then P.S. 5, then Spire Junior High School, a sort of rapid advance school for the intellectually bright children. It's an experimental school connected with Columbia University. After that it was the DeWitt Clinton High School, then the Juilliard School of Music for my Bachelor's degree, and Columbia University for my Master of Arts. I continued working on in education, seeking my doctorate at Columbia. But they wanted me to publish my own thesis, which would have cost about two thousand dollars. I just buckled at that. That was the final slap in the face. I had been slapped in the face enough as a Negro in education in America and I had had enough hours and days of raising my hand with the answer and the teacher looking around the room and simply not seeing my hand. I'm dark brown. When I raise my hand you can't help seeing it. I wasn't a ghost. And there were many, many instances of overt discrimination.

Q: *Did you ever encounter the reaction that Negroes should not be interested in opera?*

No. Not that. I remember one class in Columbia University. I think I was speaking about why I didn't like opera, citing such things as one character, becoming angry, and raising his knife to kill another, and then holding it there for three minutes while he sings his aria! That just didn't work out for *me*. I felt that there must be some way of making opera more realistic. The teacher sat back and very coldly went at me saying "life and the world is not bounded by the Harlem River on the East Side and the Hudson River on the West Side, McCoomb's Dam or whatever it is on the north and the Bowery on the south—there *are* other horizons." He kept talking, I couldn't interrupt and I couldn't answer back. It was personally damaging that he should accuse me of having a limited horizon because I didn't like opera. I said that I didn't like it because the action was too far away from where it should be at a given moment. But he didn't catch that at all.

Eventually, after I started conducting and began to be known, he sent me a very sweet letter, mentioning nothing about that, but with one of his scores saying that maybe I would possibly be interested in performing it.

Q: *You always wanted to conduct?*

No. I wanted to play ball, to go running with other boys, talk with the girls and so forth. But then I had been coming along on the violin from the age of three and a half, for the teacher came a few weeks after the incident I described with the dining table, and I got a right-sized violin, but I hated it. I did everything in my power to stop practicing, but I was kept at it. Then at the age of nine I began playing on the radio in New York. I had accomplished that much on the violin. My playmates, who had been laughing at me and calling me a sissy, began to ask whether they could take my violin case while we went into the radio station. Radio was so new then that it was still a crystal set. (I was born in 1915.) So that began to have a status symbolism. I said, well, maybe this thing is not so bad. There might be something in this violin gig, said I to me. Then in junior high school and high school, by virtue of my playing in the school band, I got a special pass to come late and leave early—they couldn't stop me. That was terrific. And then when they had these big class nights we sat down in the pit so we could see the whole audience and it began to have special attributes that were profitable. Then when I was ready to leave high school, my parents felt that I should become a doctor. Actually, a baby specialist. McGill University was already picked out for me. It was all programmed.

Their idea in keeping me behind the music so diligently, until I took over and became my own diligence, was that because I had asthma—I can still develop a nice case of it under the proper circumstances—it was my family's idea that with inclement weather and with the racial situation in America, I wouldn't have to be begging for a job if I tried to get my education, but that I could start teaching. I could sit at home and my money would come to me—I would teach music. And therefore, if I had a big attack of asthma and I stayed home and stayed warm and dry for five days, I could earn money for those five days without being exposed to the weather.

So that on the basis of that, when I was ready to leave high school, to be shipped off to premed or whatever it was at that time before premed, the head of the music department at Clinton High School asked to see my parents. He sat down and said, "What are you going to do with his musical talent, throw it away in medicine?" And he gave me a note to Walter Damrosch who was the head of the Institute of Musical Art of the Juilliard School of Music— there were two schools at that time—and I started there as a violin major. My family felt that with all of this investment of time and patience and money and work, if anything happened to one of those five fingers, it would be too bad. So they reasoned that maybe if I had some degrees behind my name and I lost both hands, I could still earn my money.

So I changed over after six months to a violin major in what they call public school music, the only degree course at the time in music—at Juilliard. In that, I began conducting. At the same time I saw the situation in Harlem, I saw the situation in America in music, and I began to hear about the unwritten law which says Negroes are not allowed in. They are not even called to audition. When Negroes in some way did get in, took the audition and passed, they were invited into the private office and asked, "If they could possibly . . . were they absolutely sure that they were Negroes, or isn't it a possibility that they were

Spanish, or Mexican, or something?" If they could discover that they were not Negroes, the job was theirs. They had a job the week after that. If they insisted they were Negroes, then it was, "Sorry, you didn't pass the audition."

I saw the situation and I had opportunities in the Juilliard School to play in the orchestra, and we would play Brahms and Haydn and Mozart and Wagner. I began getting a repertoire. I was living in the musical life. Before that, I had been playing in orchestras—the DeWitt Clinton High School orchestra—every Thursday night, every Friday night, all day Saturday, all day Sunday. There was a group of us who used to go from orchestra to orchestra, building up our experience to get into the profession. Never did I meet another Negro on any of these trips. I remember sessions in particular at the Von Steuben Society in Yorktown, the German section in New York. There I was, playing in the Von Steuben Society orchestra and this went on day after day, and I had tremendous experience by that time, but I wasn't meeting any Negroes in these areas.

At this time the NAACP and the Urban League were beginning to sharpen the teeth of the Fair Employment Practice Committee approach and beginning to ask for other antibias legislation. It struck me even at that early age that when they finally open the doors and say, "All right, fine, we don't want to have any trouble—there's a place for violinists, please bring us a Negro violinist, we'll let him play and we'll see what happens," then suddenly we're going to grab these Negro violinists from the Apollo Theater on 125th Street who play nothing but oompa, oompa, oompa and jazz and then suddenly send them up to take a symphonic audition—this is crazy! They'll never get in. And it will put everybody back another twenty-five years. I felt what we needed in Harlem was a symphony orchestra. If once a week at least, Sunday morning, anytime, these men had a chance to go through the symphonic literature, at least they'd know the difference between the jazz rhythms they are playing and the way Beethoven writes the same rhythm and the way you have to play it differently.

So I started an orchestra in Harlem in 1932. And that went on. I continued my work at the Juilliard School. I had started teaching at the age of thirteen already. That's the way I paid for my schooling. I started the orchestra in thirty-two in the local YMCA with two of my pupils, a piano pupil and a violin pupil, and I was conductor. I called it the Dean Dixon Symphony Orchestra right away because I didn't want to go up through the words "trio," "quartet," "quintet," "sextet," and so on. I knew I would run out of words when we got to the eleventh or twelfth. And eventually we did, we had about ninety-five members when we finished. The Dean Dixon Symphony ended in about forty-two or forty-three and by that time we'd played in forty special concerts.

After a lot of struggling in America, I decided to come to Europe, where I felt I could make some progress. Since 1949 I've conducted in a number of cities all over the continent and, though I've had to overcome certain European prejudices about Negro conductors, I've done quite well.

Wherever I've gone—and I've been in many cities in Europe—I've received an enthusiastic reception from the people. I think that Italy was probably the place where I received one of my warmest responses from audiences. My wife and I lived in Italy for a while and it is one of my favorite places. I like the Italian outlook on life—indeed, I like the European *style.*

Q: *Was there any legacy of racial attitudes in Italy, attitudes hung over from their war against the Ethiopians there?*

No, we seldom found that in Italy at all. The places in

which we found prejudice or racism in Italy were where their clientele had been or still was primarily American. In order to keep the American dollars, since they had heard so much of "if they let a Negro into this place, then I won't come back," it was much easier for them to keep Negroes out.

But this was not a general rule in other countries. We found bias in a restaurant, in a big hotel in Malmö, Sweden, where there are not more Americans than anywhere else. It's not an American town or an American hotel. But I do much conducting in Sweden. I first conducted in Göteborg in fifty-two; then from fifty-four I was head conductor of the Göteborg Symphony until sixty. I did much work in Stockholm and Malmö, and it was during a period in Malmö that we went into a restaurant and an American there called over the headwaiter when he saw us enter and said, "Please get rid of that man. If he stays, I don't stay!" The headwaiter immediately said to him, "*You'll* have to leave. You have made yourself unwanted." So *he* had to leave. We didn't hear about it for a long time, maybe two years later.

That didn't happen to our faces. But other things have. Once we got on the ferry between Copenhagen and Malmö and we came in a party; the two of us, our three children, and a maid. We walked up to the first-class restaurant (we had first-class tickets) and my wife asked for a table for six. The waiter takes a quick look and says, "We have no place." So I said, "How come?" because we were very early. "I don't serve Negroes," says he. I said, "You wait," and dashed up to the captain. The captain was enraged. The ferry was delayed for half an hour, there was a big scene, and the fellow was kicked out. So you see, in Europe the Negro can win sometimes.

Where do I think he got that attitude from? Where do

you get the phrase, "We don't serve Negroes," except from Americans? I haven't heard it any place else in the world. I don't think they have the phrase, even in South Africa. I think the Africans in South Africa are so conditioned that they know where not to go to raise the question.

Q: *What about in Australia?*

Australia has been without one iota of prejudice toward me, in any sense. I'm an honorary Aryan, I guess. I'm chief conductor with the Sydney Orchestra and I conduct there three and a half months a year.

Q: *Have you been back to America in recent years?*

I went back in fifty-two. I left in forty-nine and I made two quick trips back afterward.

Q: *Did you conduct on either occasion?*

No.

Q: *Are there any Negroes who conduct major orchestras in the States?*

I don't know, I don't keep abreast of it. But I have a tendency to doubt it because I think that anyone who does rise up high enough will become internationally famous, and I would have heard.

Q: *Then things haven't changed materially since you were there?*

Not that I know of. I have first-hand knowledge from fellow Negro musicians with whom I speak when we meet somewhere and from many students and young professionals who write me letters, long, pitiful letters, asking my advice about what they should do. A couple of months ago I received a letter from a Midwestern boy who says that he knows his heart is in music, his heart is in conducting, he *wants* to conduct, he *knows* he can conduct, but his parents say that there is no future in conducting for a Negro. They refuse to let him go into it because they feel that it's a dead end. I haven't answered it yet, I'm a little behind in my mail. I plan to tell him that I don't agree with his parents at all.

There *is* an opportunity, absolutely, especially with the world becoming as small as it is, distance-wise, time-wise. If he has any real conducting talent, there absolutely is a possibility for him. But I say that he must himself under-stand—and get his parents to understand—that America is not the only horizon to look toward. If some opportunities in America don't exist as yet then he must go where they do exist. He can't think of America only. By virtue of my being what I am here and in Australia, at least these two places have been opened to black conductors and Germany means all of Europe. Because when any Negro announces himself as a candidate for a position or a job or a guest conductor's spot in Europe today, he does it against the background of the reputation that I have established. That reputation is good, so his chances of being accepted now are that much greater.

I feel that my role has been, since the emergence of the American Negro, to make as many successes as possible. Because those successes mean that when the next Negro comes along, he won't get the rebuffs that I got; there won't be "Oh, we couldn't do that—we've never done it!" A new tradition has begun. In Sweden, when I first went to Stockholm, a Swedish orchestra was asked about having me as a guest conductor, and the answer was, "Well, if he will do it in white-face with white gloves on, then it's all right." One year later they asked me to be their conductor. I started in sixty here in Frankfurt but I started in Germany in 1954 at Baden-Baden—between 1951 and 1960 whenever Holland was offered my services, the re-action was "Ugh! We can't afford to have a circus!" So Holland was blocked until I went there for the first time, but it has gone very well after that.

One of the last countries in Europe to take down the pillars of prejudice in music was Switzerland. About four years ago even they opened up and asked me to come.

Q: *Do you feel you could live in the States again?*

No, no, no, no, no. I think I could *visit* the States, and it is one of my deepest desires to visit America as a guest conductor or with my own orchestra, preferably with my own orchestra. If the conditions were right, I would even consider it as a guest conductor. But this would be in order to balance the scales, to set the record straight for all those who said it couldn't happen and for the people in America who said, "No, I won't come to a concert conducted by a Negro conductor because there's no such thing." For all of those and for that kind of feeling, I would come back. Mainly, I would go back to show our own people—Negroes —that I *do* exist, that it is not completely lost, and that the lies spread about our intellectual inferiority, and the myth that only jazz can come out of us really is a myth. We haven't yet had a concert pianist of international reputation, we've only had singers and, according to whites, singers are merely "a gift of God," like our athletes in sports. So to help my people get some more basic faith in the possibility of achievement, that it *can* exist against the odds that they know too well, I would perform in the States. I wasn't born in Europe and I haven't had the benefits that so many people from Belgium, Luxembourg, Paris, Italy and Scandinavia have; once people in those countries raise a local son who has some talent, they're all behind him, he gets everything he needs. Americans don't do this, not even for whites. That is, unless you get into certain musical cliques, but that's different. That's very special. But I didn't have this. I was an expatriate. I had kicked myself out of America, and even if I hadn't they weren't interested in helping me. Because helping an

American Negro *in my field,* a field which requires a certain intellectual background, which requires organizational ability, which requires a *leadership* ability, goes against what America says we Negroes don't possess. We're not supposed to have these qualities. Therefore, once they present me as a respected conductor, that gives the lie to those things they are saying behind our backs all the time. The lie they use in Congress as the reason for giving less money for Negro education than for white education. So for all of these reasons I have a great desire to come back to America, but I don't come back as a *Negro* conductor, I come back as an *international* conductor.

Arthur Hardie:

STOCKHOLM

"Some fellow, a Swedish-American journalist, was over here trying to do an article on American Negro writers, painters, playboys and all that, but I didn't want to get involved," Arthur Hardie, a black painter in Stockholm, told me when we met, after questioning me closely about my objectives. "Certain things are negative as far as I'm concerned," he explained. "This cat wanted to have a party with some of us Negroes and a lot of Swedish girls and all that kind of thing. I'm not against a party, mind you, but if someone makes a story out of that and puts it into the wrong medium, it just makes some people angry, other people disgusted and it doesn't do anything good for anybody."

Arthur Hardie works hard at his painting and, like a dozen or so other black artists, finds Scandinavia a fruitful place to labor. The fact the visiting writer had wanted to exploit with his "party" was the fascination many Scandi-

navians have with black folk. To a people whose lives are comfortable but dull, the black man brings a touch of the exotic, his skin evokes images of warmer climes and primitive passions. Girls in the streets turn aside from their blond male companions as the dark stranger passes, mixing curious stares with measuring glances. While all black peoples are a novelty to the Nordics, the background of the American Negro with his Little Rocks, Selmas and Watts is of special interest. With a dearth of emotional crises in their own societies, Scandinavians find in the civil rights struggle in the U.S. a cause to enlist their ardent sympathies and financial support.

To Arthur Hardie and other black expatriates, on the other hand, Scandinavia offers a chance to see if the obstacle in the U.S. was color or competence, in an atmosphere which allows for their difference.

Arthur Hardie

I came from New York. I attended a boarding school there for several years, then went to Cardinal Hayes High School and was graduated from Commercial Art School. That was in 1948. But I had studied with an artist since I was about seven or eight years old.

Was my life in America tough? Not comparatively. Knowing what I know today, I'm sure my life was not as tough as many. I was sort of sheltered, particularly in boarding school. When I came out of that school I couldn't believe all the things I'd heard about the cops, for example. Other colored people told me about things that were happening in the South and I just couldn't believe them.

After I got into high school I learned that all the things I had thought were exaggerations were true. I won't say I got bitter, but I sure got *wiser*. I didn't have any really bad experiences, but I had the usual job interviews where they gave you all kinds of reasons for not giving you the job.

For a while I wanted to be an engineer because I liked anything electronic and I used to fool around with radios and other devices, but once I really looked into it, I realized it meant more than just being handy with your hands, that a lot of special background was needed.

I never was involved in civil rights activity as such; in fact, there wasn't any kind of civil rights stuff *then*. I belonged to the NAACP, of course, but I have never felt I was able to make a real contribution in any of the groups that I belonged to because the individual gets swallowed up. I didn't feel that I could express what *I* feel in an organization.

I had a jewelry store on Forty-third Street between Fifth and Sixth avenues for three years and ninety-nine per cent of the people I was dealing with were white. When I was in boarding school all the students were Negroes but all the nuns who ran it were white. So you might say I have always been involved with whites in some way.

My first encounter with Europe was in 1951 when I was twenty-one and in the Army. I was in Paris for four months after sort of cutting out on the Army. I went back to the Army, stayed there for another four months and then I got out of *that*. It's hard to explain because so many things happened but it had to do with the way I saw the war itself. I was to be sent to fight Koreans and I couldn't see where there were any differences between Koreans and *me*. It would be the same thing if I were in America today and were going to be sent to Vietnam. *I* don't have anything against the Vietnamese and I'm sure I wouldn't have any trouble getting along with them. I'm not anti-Communist or anti-American. I'm not anti-anything. I'm just for the bigger thing, humanity, which seems to be disappearing these days.

I came back to Europe in 1960 and I've been here ever since. I guess I left America because I didn't always want to have to be proving I was as good as white people. As I've told you, my situation threw me in with whites almost all the time. But in restaurants, on jobs, or even at parties, I always felt that they were weighing me. I decided it was better to live someplace else for a while, even if I did not stay, so that I could evaluate myself in a neutral situation. In America, the pressures against you prevent you from getting a good picture of what you are. Every time you see another Negro, you see how he has been repressed and you see how you have to fight the image you have been given of yourself. Young Negroes today realize this same thing—because a lot of things have happened among Negroes since I was fighting with this—but at that time I felt I had to leave *that*. You get to the point where it's hard to go beyond the things society is constantly telling you about yourself. You get to the point where you're just operating on faith.

You get up in the morning and go to apply for a job and The Man turns you down with some excuse and it's hard to keep believing that what you think about your worth is really true. You become bitter and that's self-defeating. You walk into every interview saying to yourself, "This cat's going to boot me."

After I got out of America and had a chance to compare societies, I lost faith in the whole American idea. It all happened over a period of time and I can't pinpoint any one thing but the idea of saluting a flag, talking about "one nation indivisible with liberty and justice for all"

just makes me have contempt for it. Because I'm not
"American" now, not in the sense that we often mean. I
think America *could* be a great country, but whether it
will or not—well, we'll see. I haven't given up my citizenship and I don't want to become a Swedish citizen either.
I'm not against either country but my attitude has to do
with war, which I'm against, and what government means,
at least to me. I prefer the Swedish way because up till now
there has not been the idea here of keeping certain groups
down the way there is in America—and even though things
are changing in America, it is still far away from being
what it is here. For example, I can go anywhere in Sweden
and not have any problems because of race. I don't have to
worry that if I go south or west or somewhere that I'm
going to have trouble. On the other hand, if I went back to
America with my wife, who's Swedish, I couldn't go any
place, hardly, outside of New York. I could make more
money in New York, and it *is* difficult earning a living as a
foreigner in Sweden. But I know that here I will always be
looked upon as an individual. I've worked here as a silver-
smith and a jewelry designer. I've met people from all
walks of life, film writers and all kinds of people whom I'd
never be able to meet in America. Peter Weiss, the play-
wright, for example, is one of my friends here.

So being here gives me the chance to do what I want to
do. When I paint a figure, nobody asks me, "Why didn't
you paint a Negro?" or anything of that kind. I don't have
to explain everything in terms of "The Negro Problem."
Most of my paintings today don't have any people in them
at all, so how can I explain "The Negro Problem" in
them? I don't say that Sweden is the best place to live in all
ways. There are a lot of things it is easier to do in America
than it is here. Americans are much more enterprising, in
the general sense. But being a Negro means I'm apart from

that "general sense." As a Negro here, I am not held back as much. On the other hand, there are individual Negroes who may be able to go much further in America than they can here. I know a fellow who's an engineer and he came here to work but he couldn't get a good enough job. He said it was because he was too young. He had been what is called a "project engineer" in America which was rather high there, but here they have a system in which you get paid according to your age also—age has something to do with your salary. So he felt it was better for him to go back to America. He was interested in racing sportscars and he felt he couldn't make enough here to be able to do that. Well, I can understand that, if that's what he wants to do. I don't say I can paint better here than in America but I *can* paint with a *freer spirit* here, nothing's forced on me. I don't feel I have to *prove* anything.

Mattiwilda Dobbs:

STOCKHOLM

Sweden, the welfare state, is not the refuge for the Negro (or anyone else) of little means. The permanently floating con game of black hipsters and hustlers one may encounter in Copenhagen, Paris or Amsterdam does not linger in Stockholm. It simply costs too much to live there. But for the Negro who can meet Sweden on his own terms, that is, with something to offer, the rewards can be satisfying. For the jazz musician, there is a respect for his music almost amounting to adoration, a homage which awards a dignity to this music's creators that they seldom receive in the States. Newspapers carry long, scholarly analyses of the works of a John Coltrane or an Ornette Coleman, sell-out audiences of well-dressed Swedes sit in rapt suspension listening to their concerts. Ex-heavyweight champion Floyd Patterson, a frequent visitor, is a folk hero there. Though he was once defeated by a Swede, Ingmar Johannsen, his self-effacing behavior appeals to the Swedes and his like-

ness is to be seen gazing lugubriously out of candy adver-
tisements all over Sweden.

What of the average, noncelebrated, just-out-of-the-
ghetto Negro? John Henry, a New Yorker, came to Sweden
as a Patterson sparring partner and stayed on to marry and
live in Stockholm. For him, life is a bittersweet amalgam
of freedom and struggle. He earns a water-line salary
which, with that of his wife's, affords him a modest flat in a
large, new, suburban apartment complex. He does not be-
lieve he'll ever make enough money to afford some of the
amenities he had in the States and he cannot adjust to the
stares of the curious or the kinds of questions he's asked by
total strangers. He broods about the possibility of coming
back to America but for his wife that is an unacceptable
solution.

Perhaps the best-known American Negro living in
Sweden is the singer Mattiwilda Dobbs. She lives in Stock-
holm where she is the wife of Bengt Janzon, head of a
Swedish public relations firm.

Mattiwilda Dobbs

Q: *Before coming here to Stockholm, you lived in*
Hamburg?

Yes, I was with the Hamburg Opera for two and a half
years. I didn't like living there. I love Sweden. I was here
before and then I went down to Hamburg because I
wanted to sing in that opera house. I traveled out from
there—I was at the Met at the same time so I was only
there part time, but we actually moved our home down
there at one point.

Q: *You say you wanted to sing at that opera house?*

Yes, I had a chance to do some interesting productions there with a famous stage director, and it's a very fine opera—the Hamburg Opera. Then I wanted to learn German and everything. I had several reasons for going. I stayed there two and one half years, but I always longed to get back to Sweden because I like it so much here. I first came to Europe when I was a student, in 1950, and I went to Paris on a scholarship. I was studying French music. I had done all my vocal studies in New York and I wanted to specialize in French repertoire. I was there for two years.

Q: *You went through school in Atlanta, your home town?*

Yes, I went to Spelman College there. But it's a long time to stay at home. I'm happy now that I did, however, because I feel you don't ever get back. I lived in Atlanta till I was twenty-one, until I finished college. Nowadays a lot of families in the South send their children away to Northern preparatory schools so they can go to the big universities; they leave home now at fourteen or fifteen years old. It's sad.

All my sisters went to Spelman. We were six in our family. I was a music major and I minored in Spanish and French because I was trying to decide whether I should be a singer or a teacher of Spanish.

Q: *How did you get launched in your profession?*

Well, when I finished college I had already started majoring in music, so I was very interested. I had taken voice lessons in college and started singing solos at school and church and then I had to decide whether I was going to go in for a teaching career or a singing career. It was mainly my father and my music teacher at school who persuaded me to start singing. I wanted to, but I was just afraid.

Q: *What did your father say about it?*

Well, he had faith in me and he definitely wanted me to try. So I went to New York and I found a very good teacher, who was a former German singer—she was a refugee.

We have a lot of fine teachers, thanks to Hitler. The Germans have lost a whole generation through the war, teachers and the singers who now would have been in their prime, who now would have been the major singers. That generation is just lost. And the new one hasn't come. That's why they don't have many native German singers who are very good. I benefited from that, I suppose, because I went to New York in 1946. My teacher had been there about eight years. At the same time, I still hadn't given up hope of being a teacher—not that I wanted to, but I wanted some insurance. I had lots of free time on my hands at first because I was only taking two voice lessons a week, so I started taking some courses at Columbia University and after two years, working part time, I got my Master's in Spanish. Fortunately, I never had to use it. But I have never regretted it. And I'm glad I used that time when I had it. It's strange how that worked out, because later on I went to Spain to live. I have lived in France, Spain, Germany, Sweden, and I have been very much in England, though I've never actually lived there.

I first came abroad in 1950, after four years' study with my teacher in New York. I felt that I was ready to try and start professionally, and it was very difficult at home. Managers don't take you on if you have no experience.

Q: *Was that the only reason you didn't start in America?*

Well, I didn't quite think I was ready either. I wanted to do a little more studying. At that time I wasn't thinking so much about opera, because no Negroes were in the Met then—though there were two at City Center. Moreover, my teacher had been a concert singer and she trained me as a concert singer. That was what I was planning on being.

Q: *Did you have a feeling for one against the other?*

I've always preferred concert singing. I really love that. So that was my personal choice, too.

Q: *What about singing in opera—had you had any discussions about that?*

Well, I studied opera. My teacher sent me to an opera workshop at the Mannes Music College in New York. I got a scholarship there and was there for two seasons, and then I was at the Columbia opera workshop; during that time I appeared in a performance which was given at the University of Michigan in their summer drama festival. It was just a student production; that was the first thing I was in. Then I studied opera at the Berkshire Music Festival. I was really planning for opera, I suppose, I can't say that I wasn't. But I was working toward concert too, but I didn't know what was going to develop.

Q: *You said there were only two Negroes at that time?*

That's right. But none at the Met. Marian Anderson was the first and that wasn't until 1955.

But to get back to why I went to Paris: I had been studying voice and since my teacher had taught me mostly German, I wanted to study French literature. I got a John Hay Whitney scholarship and went to study in Paris for two years. Actually I had another objective in going to Paris—to try and start singing in Europe. I somehow thought I might have a better chance there because you know Europe is more willing to give unknown artists a chance than America is.

Q: *You mean just "unknown"?*

Oh, you mean does color come into it? I really don't think so, because there was a lot of opportunity in concerts for Negro singers, though not so much in opera.

Q: *But opera was important to you?*

Yes. But I really didn't have much hope for opera then. It had been closed in America and up until that time I had never heard of Negroes singing in opera in Europe either. There was certainly nobody in recent times. I hoped to start concert work in Europe and then come back home.

I had been in contact with a manager in New York. He had not been able to do anything for me. But he did put me in contact with a manager in Paris, and I sang for that manager when I went to Paris. At the time he didn't think he could do much for me. It was only after I had won a prize in the Geneva Conservatory of Music in 1951 at an International Competition that this manager was able to work something out, and he got me one or two concerts in Paris with orchestra—my first engagement was in the performance of *The Messiah* in a big concert hall in Paris, sponsored by the American and English churches.

The prize I won attracts quite a bit of attention from impresarios and opera managers and carries a lot of prestige. Some very outstanding singers have won it in the past. You have to be ready to start your career—and it's very competitive. As a result of the prize I got my big break—I was asked to go to La Scala and sing for them. There had never been any Negroes at La Scala. One of the judges from the contest had told them about me, and I got a letter from them asking me to come down. I made my debut there in a Rossini opera with an Italian conductor.

Just before I got the prize I had decided I was going to try to give a couple of concerts myself, because I had some money left over from my scholarship. I had gotten three thousand dollars and people had told me if you presented yourself in a concert—it wouldn't cost much because the rental of a hall would be two hundred or three hundred dollars—the critics would come. So I thought I would do it in Paris, but everybody said that would be too expensive; it was too big a place and you don't get much chance for engagements afterward if you are unknown. They advised me to go to The Hague, where you get the same press but can do it more cheaply, because it's smaller. For two hundred dollars I went there and sponsored myself in a recital and I got very good reviews. While I was there, the manager that I had paid to arrange the concert asked me to stay and sing for the director of the Holland Festival, and I did. Then the next year I heard from him and he offered me the leading role in an opera by Stravinsky which was going to be done during the Holland Festival in 1952. That was my absolutely first opera.

Then, after La Scala in 1953, I had all kinds of engagements, because I got a lot of publicity both here and in America, in *Time* Magazine and elsewhere, that attracted Sol Hurok, whom I met in Paris. I sang for him there and he gave me a contract and took me to the States in 1954. Then I had a Town Hall debut and a concert. Everything went quickly from then on, after La Scala.

Q: *Any special reason for coming to Stockholm?*

Well, I heard that Scandinavia was good for artists, that they paid well and they had a lot of work. So I got a lot of work in Holland and a lot of work here. I made five trips here before I met my husband, so as you can see I've been here many times.

They have a lot of summer work here in the folk parks; they have opera singers and concerts, all kinds of things for the people. It's a very good system and it employs a lot of artists. My first engagement was a tour for the parks and I came here for that. Then later I came for concerts and things. It was on my sixth trip here, in 1957, that I sang in the opera for the first time here. My husband, who was a journalist and used to have columns in *Svenska Dagbladet* and *Expressen* at that time, did public relations for the opera.

My husband used to be in films—that was his first career—he's had a lot of different ones; they have all been very helpful in building him up. But they have also been very helpful for me because he was my manager. Now he's retired from managing me. He has been a producer, a PR man with Paramount Pictures, a columnist, then he was with the opera and now he has his own PR firm. He also had a very popular radio program during the time he had the column. His column was something like Earl Wilson's, but not only about theatrical people. About politicians and everybody. His program went on in the morning. It was called "Alarm Clock" and it was the second most popular program in Sweden. He was the first one to call up people—this was in the 1940's—and talk to them on the phone, on the air. This was something he had learned in the States. He had lived in the States for four years.

I think the one thing that helped to bring us together was the fact that my husband had lived in America and knew Americans and that I had lived in Europe so long. I really feel more at home here; I've been away fifteen years now. That's a long time. I go back every year but I have never moved back. I feel most at home here in Sweden because my husband lives here and I have been here off and on for eight years. I think Sweden is a perfect combination; it has the best of Europe and the best of America. It has a very high standard of living and the people are also interested in the cultural things that Europe has. I think they have the best of the efficiency and progressiveness of America combined with the fine old qualities of Europe.

Q: *Are Swedish people difficult to get to know?*

Maybe, I don't know. It's been easy for me because my husband is very well known, has many friends and is the type of person who is very outgoing and makes friends easily. To come here in that kind of a situation and just have it handed to me on a silver platter is entirely different than if I had come here with an American husband and we were two foreigners. It's much easier when you marry a person here . . . in fact, before I met him, I was really ready to go back home to live because I was tired of being a foreigner and not having any roots. The only reason I continued to stay in Europe was because I met him. When we lived in Germany, one reason I didn't like it was because we were both foreigners there. I like it much better here because I can come into the country with some roots, as it were, being married to a native. It's fine to knock around when you're young but later on you want to settle down.

Q: *How does an American Negro feel in Germany?*

I was very prejudiced against Germany when I went there. I was drawn between two things: I hated Germany for the racial things they did during the war and was prepared not to like the German people. On the other hand, I admired very much their musical ability and love of music because they were among the greatest in the world in that sphere. I had thought they were really strange people. Much to my surprise, I found I liked them.

When we lived in Hamburg I got to know the German people for the first time and I found that they were kind, almost sentimental, very friendly.

Q: *Do you think Hamburg is typical?*

No, Hamburg has a very liberal history. It's a seaport and always has had people from different nations coming in and out. They've been independent in Hamburg. It was and is a free state, a city-state, and Hitler never had much success there.

Q: *Were you aware of any racial prejudice there?*

No, and don't think I'm not conscious of those things because, having been brought up in the South, I'm very sensitive to them. I remember when I was living in New York, being brushed off, you know, you are very sensitive to those things. But really, as long as I have been in Europe I have not knowingly run into any prejudice.

Q: *Do you think it was because you were a celebrity?*

Well, that may be, because in almost every country I've visited, I've been there in a professional way, and that may have made it easier for me than it would have been for a person who didn't have that. I do know, however, that in many places I was unknown to the people and I still didn't feel it. The only thing I felt in Germany was—when you talk to the people, they have a *consciousness* of race; I mean, you hear more talk about it than you do in other places. They don't dare say anything prejudiced about you, they're so sensitive. In fact, they go just the other way. You can see they feel guilty and they wouldn't dare say anything to you about the Jewish people or about the Negro race. It's just that in Germany I was more conscious of being a Negro, it was something intangible, nothing they ever said. In most other countries, I really forgot I was colored—you just do forget, you become an individual, which is what every Negro wants.

Q: *And the Germans never said anything about Jews in your presence?*

No, only one time. There was a little girl who was a fan of mine, she was only seventeen. She used to come backstage and ask for my autograph. When I had a concert in England she was there at the time, living with friends to learn English, and she came to my concert. My agent, a

Jewish refugee from Vienna, drove me to my hotel and was taking her to the subway. The girl was talking about the family she lived with and all of a sudden she said, "They're Jewish and I don't like living with Jews!" That was terrible, especially in a person so young. I had felt that young people were not like that. In Germany, I suspected everybody over forty years old; they were guilty until proved innocent. Still, on the other hand, I liked them. I must say, in no other country, even in Italy, is the opera singer looked up to as in Germany.

Q: *What did it first feel like when you came to Europe?*

I had felt segregation more in New York than I had in the South but Europe never gave me that feeling. I had expected much more of the North. But you had to worry about a restaurant waiter putting you at a back table and you always wondered, "Can I go into this restaurant?" In the South you live on your own little side and you don't come into situations where you can really be hurt.

I get such a rude shock when I go back to America because I forget. I'm much more sensitive to it now because I'm no longer used to it. One thing that surprised me when my husband and I went to New York the last time was how people stared. Now, you wouldn't think people would stare like that!

Q: *Do they stare at you here?*

No. It's not in the nature of a Swedish person to stare. They're very well bred and they don't allow their children to gape at you. They tell them, "Don't stare." When you go to Latin countries you do have a lot of staring, especially a few years ago. One time in Spain at a bull fight—I was there with my sister in 1951—they were actually holding up children to get a better look at us!

In New York they stare at interracial couples, angry stares, and it surprised me. My husband got very angry and he wanted to say something to some of them but I restrained him.

We were married in New York and we spent every winter in New York for about six years. I had been married before. When I was a student in Paris I met another student there, a Spaniard, studying at the Sorbonne. We married but that marriage was very short for he died one year later. My career was just starting then and we moved from Paris to Madrid. After he died, I really decided to move back home. I was actually spending a lot of time in America. I wasn't in the Met then but I had concerts there and I had a lot of work, so I was on the go all the time. When I was in the States I was either with my parents in Atlanta or with my sister in New York, so I really didn't need any type of apartment in America. I kept my place in Madrid to have an apartment in Europe to come back to. I was in Madrid when I came to sing at that first concert and met my present husband and then I moved up here.

Q: *What did you feel, when you first came to Paris?*

Oh, it was a great feeling, it really was. To be young and to be a student in Paris, that's one of the nicest things that could ever happen to anybody. I think that those were wonderful years. It had nothing to do with being colored, it was just nice. But of course it *was* a freedom. And it was a relief from prejudice which I had never experienced before—just to be able to forget all about it. I loved the liberal experience in France, not only for race, but for everything, the wonderful spirit of freedom. They really believed in "live and let live."

Q: *Did you have to make any adjustments in your own thinking?*

As a Negro? No, I think that's something that comes easily to you. I would never expect anything like that in

France, people have always been wonderful. And one thing . . . one reason I really wanted to go there was because I had an older sister who had been in France in the thirties on a scholarship, she had been a teacher of French. When I was a little girl she used to write home about this. I suppose that had something to do with it. But I *was* a little disappointed in the French people in that they were hard to get to know. I met very few. All my friends were foreigners. I had some American friends, though not many *white* Americans. I know I'm wrong, but I shirk white Americans in Europe. I was wondering if *you* were going to be white or colored. I was very happy when I saw that you were colored. But I know that's wrong.

I know it's very wrong because I have met some very nice white Americans. I have a problem, you see, because as I told you my husband is very friendly and outgoing. He lived in America and he likes Americans very much. Naturally, when he meets Americans, he always wants to be friendly with them. *I'm* always kind of scared. But through him I have met some very nice people.

Q: *When you go back to the States, how do you feel?*

It was a peculiar situation. You see, now my father's dead, but when we first married my family home was still intact and I wanted to take my husband down to Georgia. That was when Atlanta was in a state of unrest and trying to decide exactly what it was going to do about integration. My father was very active in getting Negroes registered to vote and he had been threatened by crackpots and fanatics who called him up in the night. My mother had heart trouble and she was so afraid that I didn't want to worry her with anything more, so I never took my husband down there. We always stayed in New York.

Q: *Do you feel more of a complete woman in Europe?*

Well . . . no. It depends on what countries you're in.

In the Latin countries women aren't as emancipated as they are in the United States—but here, this is a great country for independent women with careers. It's a funny thing; I love the Swedish people and I get along with them very well. But the Spanish people are more like *Negroes*. I speak Spanish—it's my best foreign language—and that helps a lot. But apart from that, I felt very much at home there. Although the type of life there was rather restricted, still I loved it. Here you encounter the Anglo-Saxon temperament, but since I'm an American Negro I can fit into either place. You have your racial temperament in Latin countries and here you have your environmental temperament. Swedes like people with different temperaments. In fact, the person who's different can fit in here very well.

Swedish people are a little like the English people in that they like foreigners but sometimes they *are* a little cold. They love to travel and go to foreign countries but they're not really happy about having a lot of foreigners come into theirs; they want to keep their country the way it is. They're very cordial, though, and I must say the reception we had here—that I had here—has been marvelous. They're very interested in the Negro problem here. I would say that if there is a place in the whole world that is free of prejudice—no place is, of course—this comes closer to it than anything I've ever seen. It really does.

When I first came to actually live here it was 1957 and there were very few Negroes here. If I saw one, I turned around to look. In fact, two fellows came running up to me and asked me if I was from *Ethiopia!* But now, especially in the summertime, when a lot of tourists and students come here, it's nothing uncommon to see a number of Negroes among the visitors. Stockholm University is nearby and people around here rent out a lot of rooms to students, some of them to colored or African students.

I was in a store here the other day and these two colored boys kept looking at me, then they came up to me and asked me if I speak English. One was a Nigerian student who had been here for three years and the other one was from Trinidad.

When I played in the opera in Oslo last year there was a colored ballet dancer there teaching choreography.

Q: *Has there been any change in the attitude of the people here since more Negroes have been coming?*

No. At least not among *my* friends. I have such wonderful friends. They are all very intelligent people and very liberal. I haven't heard anything. I know that when the African students arrive, they rent rooms here and I don't think they have any difficulty.

The whole attitude here is very pro-Negro. Swedish people always take up for the underdog. They don't have any here so they look for them. They're always raising money for children in Korea and Ethiopia and different places.

Q: *Do you find tranquillity here, a slower pace than the American tempo?*

Oh, yes, I always liked that about Europe. I had three reasons for wanting to come and live in Europe. The main one was for my career; it was very advantageous for a singer to live in Europe, more opportunities, the whole climate is better for a singer or any kind of artist than in America. The second reason was that I liked the European way of life. I think a lot of it has to do with the stage at which you come. If you come at an early age, your most formative years, then it's easier to adapt than if you come later on. The third reason was the color factor. It was important, but it was kind of a dividend which was pleasant, but was not my main reason for coming here. I wouldn't leave America just because of the problem. In fact, I know a lot of American Negroes who criticize those who leave the problem, for running away.

Q: *How do you feel about that?*

Well, I think you've got your own life to live and I don't think you should choose your place to live just on the basis of color. To stay in America and fight for your race or go to Europe to get away from it; I don't think that should be your main thing. You should have other things in life, as a human being, that you put before race. I think above everything else you should be a human being, that you put before race. Racial considerations come in later. You should choose where you want to live according to what's best for *you,* whether you like it there, whether there's more opportunity there. Of course, after I married, my marriage was the decisive factor.

Q: *Do you ever feel like you should be in America at this point in history?*

Well, I *do* feel left out. There are so many wonderful things going on, so many ways in which we can help. But I don't really feel cut off from America like most exiles. I have my career in America, too, and I go back every year to sing there. I spend from two to five months in America every year. I just felt that I could do more for my race and my people by doing the best I could in my career. I thought that was my best way to contribute.

Q: *Do you come into contact with American Negroes very often?*

I only know one Negro couple in Sweden. I do miss colored people very much. Naturally you miss your own people.

Q: *Do you ever miss the kind of tension that goes with life in America?*

No, I get enough of that when I go to New York to last me the rest of the year. You know, my career is awfully competitive; I get enough in my career too. My husband's career also has a lot of tension. Sweden is losing a lot of its tranquillity. Unfortunately, the people are becoming Americanized. Sweden is so small and they have so few people that the people tend to be very efficient and highly trained, very specialized. I think it is harder and harder now for a young person who wants to make a career. It's difficult to get into medical schools. You have to have excellent grades. It's very hard because they want that high standard. The only way they can compete in the world market is through superiority and being efficient, so they have to have the best.

Still, they are becoming more American. At first the great foreign influence on Swedish culture was France. All their royalty used to speak French. Then another great influence was Germany. One of the first missionaries to Christianize Sweden was German and the missionaries taught the Swedish to read and write. There are a lot of German merchants living here. The English also had a great influence on them. They admired the English very much and emulated English fashions. But now the great influence is American. Well, I suppose, in a technical world, America is the ideal.

Diane Gray:

STOCKHOLM

*For many an Afro-American, perhaps the biggest
impact of his move to a new land is the discovery that, to
many foreigners, his black skin is desirable. What had been
stigma in America becomes stylish in Europe. Nowhere is
this more true than in the Scandinavian countries.*

*There are any number of possible reactions to this fact
for the Negro. He can use his blackness as others do their
whiteness, or their femininity, or their masculine good
looks—to gain some end that he might otherwise not obtain. He can ignore the magnetism his darkness exerts on
the Scandinavians and pretend he's just another American
in their midst. Or he can accept their sympathy as well
meant and try to establish his real identity as something
other than just an object of oppression.*

*Like other reactions to symbols, the emotional response
of the Scandinavian to the black expatriate as an escaped
lynchee makes it difficult for a Negro to explain the sub-*

tleties and convolutions of the very condition—the American Negro's—that the foreigner seeks to understand.

There is another, sometimes amusing, sometimes exasperating twist to this European vision of the primeval Negro. To many Europeans, a Negro's urbanity is seen as a thin veneer covering dizzying depths of sexuality and emotion, feelings that they—the Europeans—have become too inhibited to express. Or so the stereotype goes. A black writer from California, living in Paris, became cozy with an attractive Swedish girl he'd met at a cocktail party. As their mutual attraction became apparent, he invited her to his apartment for drinks and the hoped-for denouement. As she curled up on his sofa with a whiskey-and-water, he slipped a Sarah Vaughn disc on the record player, then stooped to unbutton her blouse. "Not now," she said huskily, "First, do your tribal *dance!"*

Diane Gray is a 23-year-old dancer who's determined that she will continue to be what she is—a black American—despite the stereotypes and the occasional misunderstandings. She lives in Helsinki, Finland, but was a guest lecturer at Stockholm's Balletakademien at the time of this interview.

Diane Gray

I left Detroit, Michigan, when I was about eighteen years old and I haven't been back since. I went to Philadelphia—to the Philadelphia Musical Academy—and directly from Philadelphia to Finland.

I learned Finnish in a month. From two children in the deep countryside. It was Finnish, Finnish, Finnish all day.

So many Americans come over and will not try to learn the local language—I didn't want to be that kind of American.

Everyone spoke English in the city, but I went to the country with a whole family of non-English-speaking people and that's the way I learned Finnish. I was teaching modern dance in Helsinki, you see, and I thought it was rather silly to have three hundred students learn English instead of my learning Finnish. So I tried to learn Finnish as quickly as I could.

My colleague Riitta Vainio and I teach together—she runs the school where I work in Helsinki—and we went to school together in Philadelphia. Her husband was on a Fulbright at the University of Pennsylvania at the time she and I were studying dance.

Later Riitta opened a dance school in Finland. It's the only school of modern dance in all of Finland and it began to get a little large, so she wrote back to the school in the States and asked for another teacher, to be chosen from among her former colleagues. She added that I was the most qualified to go. So on the Fourth of July I arrived in Finland and we started working immediately.

There was another Negro girl, Tracey Simpson, from Los Angeles, working at Marrimekko, the Finnish dress-making company. (The owner of that firm is the woman I call my godmother.) So Tracey and I became friends. I remember it was so funny to see a Negro because I had been going around for about a month without seeing any. When we first met, Tracey and I sort of stared at each other. Our hair was wild because we didn't know how to fix it ourselves. Back in the States, we were used to going to a beauty shop all the time. So when we saw each other in the street in Finland, we looked and then we laughed like crazy: "Wow! *Another one!!!*" We became friends immediately. But we still were friends with everyone else. The Finnish people are the nicest I've ever met in my life.

I've been in Denmark, too. But it's not quite the same thing as Finland. The Danes are very sensitive people. The Finns work like dogs and they'll stick with you to the very end.

I was supposed to stay for a year and I've stayed for three. Now I'm getting a little homesick because, after all, there's no place like home. Besides, I haven't really danced yet *in America,* and I want to go back.

At the school in Finland I worked usually from nine o'clock in the morning until approximately seven o'clock at night for less than two hundred dollars a month. But it didn't matter. I was teaching, and performing in television and theater. I taught both children's and adults' classes. Some were sort of creative dance, some were working with professional students who want to become dancers and some were just helping the little fat ladies reduce. From nine in the morning until seven or eight at night, every day except Saturday. Saturday it was from nine to five.

I've been here in Sweden for the last year. I've just come back from Finland, where I taught a short course, but my connections there are still good. My passport has a working visa so I can always go back and forth. The Finns granted it to me so I can go back even though I'm not working there now. I'm even in the Finnish encyclopedia, as a pioneer of modern dance in Finland!

There was no modern dance before Riitta opened her school. It was the first school of modern dance in Finland, and I was the first foreign teacher.

Not much happens at night in Finland. It's dead. But it doesn't matter, because you can stay home and have just as much fun. I go to saunas a lot and all that. We have one in our house—I use it every night when I'm there.

Do Finnish guys find me more attractive than their own girls? Yes, there's some sort of physical thing, because I am brown and everybody else here is white. It's a normal reaction. In Finland I was stared at, and at first I was flattered, and then annoyed, and then flattered again. But I decided to accept it because in Finland they very seldom see a Negro. For maybe years they won't see one except on television. And so to see one so close, for them it's really something! When you're a Negro living in an all-white country, you can understand that reaction. Just as when Tracey and I first saw each other, we ran to each other and said, "Hey!" And *we* had just left America a month previously! At first I had thought, "Everybody is looking at me!" Then, next, "Why are they looking at me?" And then later it was, "Hah, they're looking, so what!"

It was kind of a shock at first to have people staring at you, but then they used to stare in New York City. Only there it was because I had long hair. A funny thing happened as I was coming over on the boat from Stockholm to Finland. My hair was long and I always wore it pulled back, New York dancerlike, with no make-up. I wear dresses with color, a lot of color, and I was traveling with a little Jewish girl. She was fourteen years old and she had wanted to come to Europe too, so I said, "Come along with me and fly home by yourself." Her parents had said O.K. Though she was a Jewish-American, she looked Italian, French or Indian, and she had long black hair. One day some students on the boat with us were trying to teach us how to speak French in one hour. Well, there was an American Southern couple across from us, and they were saying, "The young one is definitely Italian but the other girl"—meaning me—"I think she's Indian!" I mean they just wouldn't let me be Negro. And they were going on and on saying, "She's speaking French, no, she's definitely not an American Negro, she doesn't have African features." And I was listening and I was so hysterical—they would just not say that I was a *Negro*. So finally I walked over to them and said, "Sorry, Detroit, Michigan—Negro!" and then walked away.

There was a standard joke at Marrimekko where I used to model dresses in the summertime for the tourists. A lady from Texas walked in and said: "Oh, it's so nice to see *our* girls over here working." I thought: "Now wait a minute, this is not going to do" because I've been a Freedom Rider and I've been in court for SNCC * and snack . . . the whole bit . . . sit-ins in Arlington, Virginia, riding to Alabama on buses—all of it. And though I was sitting there in Finland, very comfortable, I was still very aware of everything that's going on, and when this woman comes in from Texas and says one of "our" girls is working here, I got a little annoyed. So I told her, "I'm sorry, I don't speak English. I'll have a girl who speaks English help you." It was our big joke.

But there *are* Finnish Negroes—"Olympic" babies, born to athletes and Finnish girls after the Olympics held in Helsinki in fifty-two. They're going on fifteen now. When I see one I say, "Hey, how are you?" Then I discover they don't speak English. So we speak in Finnish and I find out their father is an American Negro or an African.

I have a friend, Marilisa Smith, who is such a girl. We looked exactly alike. The same skin. Some features alike. She is about thirteen years old. But when she first saw me she asked me to tell her all about American Negroes. She went into everything about them. I'm giving her books to read, but they're all in English and she doesn't speak or

* SNCC, the Student Non-Violent Coordinating Committee.

read any English at all. She was quite curious about me. How did I get here? Was I American? She had the same reaction as the other Finnish people because *she* had never seen Negroes. And she was stared at, herself, as a child, always. She spoke Finnish all her life, but they didn't always understand why she spoke Finnish, even in the schools when she first began.

To go back to my own situation, I don't think I'm sought out more as a Negro. I have my own group of friends. I was with a very mixed foreign group. They were Polish and Swiss and African and all mixed together, in Finland.

Finnish boys are much more courteous than American boys. I got so used to having doors opened for me and coats put on me and cigarettes lighted for me. I had one friend who used to tie flowers on my door to welcome me home when I had been away on a trip. Everyone is courteous. When people came to visit me in Finland the first time they always brought flowers or candy. You know, going out somewhere and having people open the door for you and take your coat off and hang it up and escort you—I was dumfounded by all of it.

Is there anything about Finnish boys that is special—any different from the Swedes? Yes, their temperaments are a little different. I have several little scars, not from my pet cats but from going out to dinner with Swedish men. I guess *I* was supposed to be dessert! It was not just with me, it's the way they are with *Swedish* girls. Swedish boys just assume, "You go out, you go to bed." They give you the same sort of chivalry at the table as the Finnish boys. But forget it, after the meal! Of course they expect me to go to bed with them because most Swedish girls do. They think I'm a nut. They say, "Why not?" But now we have this sort of agreement that dinner's dinner and that's it!

There's an old Swedish saying, "Thank you for the coffee," "*Tak for cafe,*" which means "Thanks for nothing, fella!"

I read more Negro authors since I've been in Europe than I did when I was in America. I read everything that I can get my hands on. I *must* read these things! I even have some Black Muslim papers sent to me even though I'm not a Muslim. Why do I feel it necessary to keep this kind of contact? So I don't forget who I am. That's all. Because it's so easy and you can get completely lost here. It's not exactly a paradise, but it's so different when you can go anywhere and be welcomed in.

When I walk with a group of Swedes across the street, and I'm walking in front, the cars stop! I would get killed in New York City trying to go across the street. They'd knock me down and anybody else! Here people let me on the bus *in front*. I'm tall and I'm skinny and I have the sort of features, I guess, which stand out in contrast to the blond, blue-eyed types.

I did have one instance of discrimination here. One time a Negro friend, Bill Caldwell, and I were dancing in a restaurant in Stockholm. There were two Swedish boys and Bill, one American white girl and myself. We were in a bar actually, and we were drinking, and Bill and I said, "Let's cha-cha." I hadn't danced with a Negro boy in so long, and I wanted to shake a little bit. I had on long boots with rubber soles and the bartender said to a boy at the bar, "Oh, look, there go two niggers, one with boots on, dancing." He said it in Swedish. And my Swedish friend—we call him the Jolly Green Giant because he's about six-five—heard him. He's not my boyfriend but he's a very good friend and we had gone out many times together. When Bill and I came back, there was sort of a big silence at the table and then the Green Giant said to the bartender,

"I think you should apologize to both of them." He repeated it: "*I think you should apologize.*" And then he said to the whole table, "Excuse me," and we thought he was going to the toilet but then he took the bartender out and beat him up. Then he said, "Now I think you should apologize." So the bartender came over and said, "I'm sorry, I had no reason to say that. I'm a little drunk, will you forgive me? Don't hold it against the place just because of me." He gave us a whole long explanation and we sort of half-heartedly accepted it. That's the only thing I can remember that happened of this kind.

Usually, I get along well with Swedish girls. One of my best friends, a very pretty Swedish girl, is one of the top coming young models here. She said that many Swedish girls won't like me. I said, "Why?" She said, "Because you're outward-going, you're warm, and they'll be jealous." I thought of what she said during an incident once in Göteborg. I was out with four Italian students, and two Swedish girls were sitting at the table nearby. They said, "Oh, what an ugly old girl she is!" And then they came into the bathroom and they were talking about me behind my back. And I grabbed them and hit them. I still have the marks on my knuckles. They were talking in Swedish, of course, but I understood every word they were saying. They said, "She must be a whore, with four men by herself," and "They come up here and take everything away from us." They were drunk. What was their reaction to my hitting them? I don't know. I left them on the floor. And walked out. I never saw them again.

What do I miss most? Finland is a little isolated, to say the least. And a kind of conversation—communication—is what I miss because I still can't really communicate with the Finns on account of I'm not a Finn. I will never communicate the same way I can with an American Negro. And that goes for every country here. You can have conversations and conversations but the same communication is not there. They don't react the same way you do to the same things. For example, they mourned Kennedy in Finland more than they did in America. Candles in every shop window, his picture with white flowers in every shop for a month. And the day of his funeral everything was closed.

But if I talk about Martin Luther King with them, they say, "Yes, he's doing good work and I believe in his point of view," but they don't *feel* his work the same way I do. If I talk about the Muslims they say, "Oh, yes, but I don't think it's fair. Why do they hate all white men?" And all that. They don't feel the same way I do. They sympathize with me when I tell them about the sit-ins or a bus ride down South, but *they* would never have to do it so they don't understand what it means.

The same direct communication I get with Negroes, I could not find anywhere in Europe, I don't think. There are certain things Negroes say together that nobody has to explain. When Tracey and I were together we spoke very precise English when we were talking to Finns as you have to, I think, in a country whose language is not English. But when we were alone, forget it! We talked the kind of talk we would have as Negroes in the States. Just being able to feel that we were still a part, that we still belonged to it. I came across the only place in Scandinavia where they had collard greens and Tracey and I had a fit! I bought about six pounds of greens. I found them in a market. They give them to the birds here. I said to the woman who was selling them, "What are those?" She said "A grade of cabbage." I said, "I would like to have them." So she gave me one stalk and I said, "I want them all." She said, "All?" So she gave me all these things. She was selling them for five cents a pound.

I also went to a slaughterhouse and got some chitlins. You can get corn meal here, from Italy, to make corn bread. It's a little coarse and you have to put a little more flour in it. I like Swedish food and I love Finnish food, but it's not *home,* it's not the same thing.

Every once in a while I get a craving. And when I do, I run right out and get some corn bread. I introduced corn bread to Finland. I came up to Helsinki with a whole case of corn meal from Stockholm. I made some one morning, as corn meal muffins for the children and they said, "What is this called, Diane?" So they started calling it "colored bread." That was a joke. They called it "Negro bread." And later there was a big article in the paper—there were "Negro recipes," "Negro bread," and barbequed spareribs, and a whole spread about it.

Do I intend to stay in Sweden? No. I have one job I'm doing, *West Side Story,* on the stage. I'm in a film, too. I made a movie here. It goes to the San Francisco Film Festival. It's called *Oi, Oi, Oi.* It's Swedish for "Oh Dear, Oh Dear." It's a modern color film where things change color, by a young director. He said he wanted me to come with him to San Francisco, with the cast, for the film festival so he could say, "See, *we* can use them!"

Clebert Ford:

ROME

In 1964, a group of black American painters working and living in Europe held a show in Copenhagen entitled "Ten American Negro Artists." In the catalogue for the exhibition one of the Negro sponsors of the show wrote: "Europe is realizing here through this exhibition an unprecedented phenomenon in art experiences. Ten Americans, not just any ten, but ten Black Americans are joined together rather far from their shores. There is something in that, I am certain, but what?"

Part of that "what," it would seem, is the need of black émigrés to communicate with each other, to draw insights and sustenance from others who have been through the American experience and who, like themselves, are forging a new existence out of which—perhaps—something important to humanity can be derived. Perhaps it is to testify to an existence beyond race, beyond nationalisms, beyond ideologies.

235

On a visit to Rome I went to the Folk Studio, a small night club offering American folk songs and spirituals whose proprietor, Harold Bradley, is a black expatriate from Cleveland. The club was packed with Italian youths who had come to hear Bradley and other Negro performers sing their earthy, mournful and joyous music. Most of the entertainers, like Bradley himself, had long been resident in Rome. Among the most popular of the songs they sang were those of the American civil rights movement, but several times during the singing of "We Shall Overcome," some of the singers faltered. I was later to discover that their vocal mishaps occurred because they had just learned the song and were not really familiar with the words! I'm sure there were young Italians in the audience who knew it better.

One powerful and sure voice in the singing group belonged to a young actor-singer-cinema-dubber named Clebert Ford. He was the club's newest recruit and it was he who had brought the civil rights songs to black Americans who had left all that behind.

Clebert Ford

I came to Europe for the first time in September of 1964. I had always wanted to come but I hadn't made up my mind whether I wanted to *live* here. This has been something that has come about within the last year. I made up my mind that I do want to stay. I decided this about six months after I arrived because by then I had begun to make a living here and that's the biggest problem for anybody who comes to Europe with the intention of staying.

As of this moment, I cannot complain about making a living. I'm not making a great living but I do work here in the area for which I'm trained and in which I have had experience—as an actor. Sometimes I also dub films and I work as a folk singer.

In the States I was an actor primarily. I did three or four Off-Broadway things, one Broadway thing and four or five television programs. Minor, as it were. I was in the New York State Fair Festival. A couple of years ago I worked in *Antony and Cleopatra,* which starred Colleen Dewhurst, and before that I did a *Romeo and Juliet* that toured the public school system in New York. Then I worked with Ossie Davis in a Broadway musical, *Ballad for Bimshire*—I took over for Godfrey Cambridge after he left—and then I worked in *The Blacks.* In fact, that's how I came to Europe—I must thank Godfrey for leaving the role so I could get it and come to Europe. I played it in New York for about a year and a half. We only played in Europe for about a week. Three days in Berlin and three days in Venice, then they all went back and I stayed on.

I was born and grew up in New York, was graduated from City College. I went the route of all actors in New York: I've worked as a schoolteacher, for the Welfare Department, for the New York State Employment Service, the post office, and God knows how many other kinds of jobs.

During the last few years I kind of made up my mind that I wanted to act. Fortunately, I was doing fairly well. The big problem is the scarcity of jobs and the ability to realize what you are capable of doing and what the market is asking for. I know, there's no doubt about it, that, as regards Negroes, there is a kind of change coming about and I know when I left several things were beginning to open up. So I really can't say I left because there was a scarcity of jobs for Negro actors—although I *can* say that for most people there is, and it's quite difficult to work regularly.

You may be familiar with LeRoi Jones' Black Arts Theater in Harlem, where they really are making an attempt to write for a Negro audience, to give Negro actors the opportunity to work in shows that essentially have what we might call a Negro kind of outlook, something Broadway does not have. In *Ballad* we tried to do what was kind of revolutionary—a kind of Negro production—which utilized Negro light men, a Negro director, and actors. It failed for any one of a number of reasons, but I think it was a good start and I would like to see that kind of thing go on.

What is the validity of a "Negro approach" to theater? Well, it's not to *acting* as such or *theater* as such. Take the Actors' Studio, for instance. They did *Blues for Mister Charlie* and Chekhov's *Three Sisters*. Now, *Blues for Mister Charlie* was the Studio's "Negro production" and utilized all the Negro actors it had. It even used actors who were not members of Actors' Studio because they needed Negro actors. But in *Three Sisters* they used no Negro actors. *Three Sisters* is a part of the theatrical literature and it does not include Negroes. I would like to feel that the time has come when *Three Sisters* can encompass Negro performers. But in terms of American thinking as of this moment, it doesn't. So I say in the place of that, then, *we* as Negroes have to develop a kind of a Negro *Three Sisters* or a Negro *Streetcar Named Desire*—not the same kind of play but a play which is as much of Negro life, let's say, as *Three Sisters* is a part of Western culture. If The Man were not discriminating there would be no need for it, but he *is* discriminating—although it may not always be a conscious kind of a thing. In the absence of a totally integrated kind of theater, there has to be another way, temporary though it might be, and as for now, I am absolutely certain that we must have, for want of another word, a *Negro* theater.

When I say I had enough work in New York, I am talking in relative terms. In relation to the amount of work that was available to actors generally, I worked. I will say this, I've been over here for eleven months and I have made almost three times as much money as I made in my last year as an actor in New York and I've worked here very regularly.

The big thing here is that you can work in several jobs at one time. I work as a folk singer, I dub films and I work as an actor. The big thing here is *survival*. Once you become kind of set up, kind of experienced and knowledgeable about the business and people know you, then you can make a living here. In other words, I have no specific commitments. I go almost from day to day. I get calls. I have a dubbing turn at two this afternoon, I worked twice yesterday as a dubber and I worked Monday as a dubber, so you find that in spite of the fact that there is no definite scheduling of work, it comes. You have enough knowledge of yourself to know that you will be called upon when there is work available. There's no dubbing in New York for whites, Negroes or anybody else. Also, there are a million folk singers in New York so there's very little outlet *there* and, most of all, there's relatively little acting.

In New York I was a member of a group called The Association for the Advancement of Negro Performers and we worked specifically to convince producers that they should utilize Negroes in "non-Negro" roles. We picketed *Subways are for Sleeping* because it was a show essentially about New York City subways and yet they didn't use any Negroes. We also picketed *How to Succeed in Business Without Really Trying*. It was a show about the Wall Street area, the financial area, and we pointed out that in spite of the fact that there are Negro office boys, Negro executives, Negro secretaries, they didn't utilize Negro performers. As a result of that picketing we got some response, and I have noticed that some of the shows are now beginning to utilize Negroes although in very small parts, in roles that I call "the non-shaker-and-mover" roles, roles that are peripheral. So there's a Negro cop, so what? They are still not utilizing Negroes in central roles. You could cast God knows how many central roles, you know, with a Negro, but as far as I can see they have not gotten around to it. They are not yet ready for it.

Here? Here is another thing and it revolves around what I kind of consider the whole different approach to Negroes here. I'm a writer, too. I wrote for a magazine in New York called *Liberator*. A very angry, virile kind of magazine. In it I've pointed out that in America the Negro is judged according to his development in the United States. So the Negro now in the States is moving toward integration and the ideal is the Negro with an education who wants to move into the white neighborhood, who wants to go to theater, who wants to be essentially middle-class.

In Europe the Negro is considered in terms of the color of his skin, his history, his realistic kind of position. What do I mean by his history? Coming from Africa, going to America as a slave, being discriminated against as a Negro —then and now. In Italy, much more so than other countries, I find the approach to the Negro is almost from a Richard Wright point of view. Watts, California, to them is the real position of the Negro in the world. So how does this relate to the theater? Here there is no attempt made to sort of back up and accept the "poor downtrodden American Negro"; here you're a Negro who has a culture that's treasured—spirituals and jazz, they love them! At Folk Studio, the Rome club featuring Negro folk singers, they go wild over these things. I have, in a sense, found my culture, by being here, because you're *black* here and there's no shame. You are what you are. In America, on the other hand, it's "Someday you'll be integrated and white enough to be accepted in the culture."

Here you don't feel ashamed of being black. I found that in America you are always faced with your "Negro-ness" and the negative reaction which that brought from the white community. It's hard to live there and to make a living there because you are always under that pressure. America is not without its compensations, I'll admit, and I'm constantly reminded of its excitement, which is what you miss here. There's always, in New York, an excitement, there's always something going on theatrically, sociologically, socially, right down the line. For those people who can kind of put up with the other things I say, all right, and I will always go back to get that kind of excitement. But for me, right now, when I'm trying to find my way as an actor, as an entertainer, Europe and particularly Rome is the place for me.

Rome does not have New York's excitement. You'll find in Berlin, for example, a kind of excitement that's almost like New York—night clubs, theater, concerts, jazz, the whole thing. Rome, on the other hand, is quite a different matter, particularly with Negroes because—well, take the Rome *Daily American* newspaper. The *Daily American* reflects the American colony in Rome which is a white upper-middle-class group. The *Daily American* is pro-Vietnam, pro-South Africa—*white* South Africa—and conservative. I remember that when Malcolm X died they ran what I consider to be a terrible editorial, vilifying the man, saying "he deserved to die, here was a man who practiced violence, preached violence. If Negroes want freedom, they must *earn* freedom"—and all that jazz. In fact, I started to write them a letter, saying, "What do you want me to do, tap dance for my freedom?" The Negroes here are entertainers, they've been here for a long time usually.

I was very discouraged when I first came here, at the lack of involvement in the Freedom Movement on the part of the Negroes I met. Not that there are that many Negroes here. It isn't too easy to make a living in this city, for Negroes or whites.

You can't help being much more concerned about Watts if you live in the States than if you live here. The primary interest here is to stay in Europe and to make a living. I have found, in Paris, Berlin and here that the Negroes who are here have either been angry enough to forget about it —the problem—or have come over and settled here because they don't want any part of it. White people here are the same way. There's one white American in the film industry who's been here for ten years and who says that he couldn't go back to the States now because things are too complex, there's too much misunderstanding, the pain of violent confrontation is almost too much for him. I feel also that many *Negroes,* if they went back, couldn't adjust to the newer, more militant, more direct kind of protest of today.

One of the things I feel about the so-called race problem is that the problem will be solved a lot easier when we ourselves understand one another. I feel the hang-up too often among black folk in the U.S. is that there has been too much of a compromise with what we might call the "White culture." I say, "Forget about the white culture." *We* have enough that is positive and exciting and quite legitimate so that we should worry about getting along with *ourselves.* I think we have a lot further to go there than trying to understand the white man, because as far as that's concerned, I *know* where he is. And I'm reminded of that, by the way, by the white tourists who come here, tourists who essentially reflect upper white middle-class America. Who gets to Rome? Rome is a city of tourists and to get to Europe costs money. One of the things I've noticed about going to the American Express office is that you don't see many Negroes there. At the beginning of the summer, millions of kids are there, but when I go to pick up my mail I don't see any "emerging Negro middle-class." On the Via Veneto also there was a time when we Roman regulars knew whenever a new Negro came into town. The word went out "through the grapevine." You can locate anybody in Rome in ten minutes, anybody at all, if he's a foreigner. It's not very difficult because Rome is such a small, provincial kind of city. You run into very few Negroes here that you don't get to know.

Do I feel any need to see Negroes? That's a good question—well, I would say I *do* miss that.

There is no Negro "community" in Rome, as such, because of the fact that everyone is so interested in *survival* that there's very little time for anything else. One *lives* here. I know a fellow who's been here eighteen years. He went back to the States and he said he was there for a week and had to leave. He was so totally adjusted to another kind of thing—his clothes, his language, the friends he had had, had all changed. I have not been back for a year but I still feel identification, and I am in communication with *Liberator* people and others, but you find that since relationships here are not affected by color at all, you can exist almost totally without a sense of color. Your friends are your friends. Whether they happen to be Italian or American. There is no consciousness of color. It's true, of course, that when white and Negro *Americans* here in Rome get together there is Watts, California, looking down your nose and an awareness of *that*. And the Italians will ask you about the Negro in America and all that, but there is not that white American sensitivity about race. There's just a direct kind of curiosity, questions such as, "You live in New York? What do you think about Watts?" I say, "Well, it's a problem," and so forth. They say, "All right, good, let's sit down and eat," and we'll have our social intercourse and that's that.

It is quite difficult to be totally free of the things one shares with one's in-group. To put yourself totally in an Italian environment. I remember when we were doing a show, we got a group of Negroes together who were Roman. I had just come from the States with a whole bunch of civil rights jokes and there was a kind of response from one guy in particular who had been over here eighteen years—"Oooooh! Yes." He hadn't heard that in a long time. The black people who are here have, I feel, given all that up. They will accept it when they face it but they are Romans now. They are Negroes who live in Rome, that's all! They speak the language, they are with Romans, they eat with Romans, live with Romans, their whole life is Roman. They know Roman music, Roman culture. They're very Italian, they're not Negro. And not American—in a sense. There will never come a time when they are completely Italian, but by and large they are out of it, as regards America.

Culturally, Italy in general and Rome in particular are very, very far behind—that's my personal opinion. In Rome, avant-garde theater doesn't exist, serious *theater* doesn't exist in Rome. The opera is here but even contemporary opera doesn't exist here. Milan is the place culturally. There are jazz, concerts, theater. Milan is the New York of Italy. I compare Rome actually with Albany, New York. It's the capital, that's all. There's nothing here but the museums, the statuary, the Pope, but the *life* of Italy does not exist here. I stay here because I make a living.

I hope to spend at least a year in the five major areas of Europe and be able to make a living, learn the language and become familiar with the country. When the time comes when I cannot make a living here, I'll move on. I'm not particularly happy with Rome, because I like theater, I like jazz, I like a night life. I'm a night person, so to speak. In New York, after theater, you went out, you had parties, sat around and discussed politics, you got *involved*, and from what I've been able to see, this does exist in Paris, in London, does exist in Scandinavia, in Berlin. But this is the one thing that Rome lacks—excitement.

Take girls. Again Rome presents a problem. Anyone will tell you—Roman, non-Roman, white or black—there is little or no area of contact, where young people of opposite sex can meet one another. There are no dances here. There are some clubs but they are *night* clubs, bars where you hang out. I have never seen more gangs. There is a song called, "All the Sad Young Men." This could really be applied to Rome. All the sad young men looking for any kind of human contact because the Roman girls are all off the street by nine o'clock.

There is very little fraternization between non-Italians and Italians. So what happens? At the height of the tourist season the Italian men are following tourist women like they were going out of existence. Italian women have made Italian men either lechers or homosexuals. Because Italian women live in their home until they're twenty-eight, thirty. They *stay at home*. There are few heterosexual relationships between unmarried people, it doesn't exist. You've got to be introduced to a girl's mother and father, be socially approved, and you have to bring her home by a ridiculous hour. There are no way-out chicks here. I've been at Folk Studio for a year and it's a kind of center for swingers, but I've yet to see Italian girls come in there alone. They always come escorted or else single girls are non-Italians. So all this means that as a single, heterosexually oriented man, I also wait for the tourists, the American girls and the non-Italian girls. *La dolce vita?* It doesn't exist. I've heard that three or four years ago, when the film was made, Rome was a wild city—now, forget it. It's a very conservative, starched, Roman Catholic city.

I have some long-range plans. In ten years or so, I hope to have completed an education either here or in the States. Then I plan to work at a Negro college, if Negro colleges exist ten years from now, as a drama coach, instructor, director. But first I want to learn the culture of Europe and, hopefully, Africa also, but I hear the hang-up in Africa—at this moment, anyway—is that the countries are not yet ready for the foreign influence in the arts, they are still developing indigenous music, indigenous theater, and one has to know the culture.

In my arguments with the black nationalists in New York I always said, "O.K., look, if you want to go back to Africa, then go!" And of course they *don't* go because then they would have to roll up their sleeves, get out there in the field, chop down the fruit and go to outhouses and really put in the work. They always copped out, saying, "Well, we're here to save the Negro in America!" Well, the Negro who stays in America wants to be an *American,* so I feel that's really a rationalization.

Going any place takes something. There are many Negroes I know who could not survive in Europe. Why? Because it requires a different outlook, particularly in Rome here. It's an easy kind of existence, appointments aren't kept here, it's a half hour and an hour late for everything. Adjusting to a new culture, a new language, a new way of looking at things—many people can't do it. You always run into people who are leaving. I know a white fellow who had been here three years who worked in films when he first came over here. When those couple of films were finished, he was through. There was no more work for him and so for the next two years after that he kind of lived on a plate of pasta, which you can do here. That's one thing about Rome, it never gets too cold, you can live here or you can get by and I know several people who are *just getting by*.

The reaction of the American Negro meeting another American Negro overseas is an interesting thing to watch. In Rome ninety per cent of the Africans I've met on the street have nodded or made some gesture of acquaintanceship. The obviously American Negro, I have found, sometimes will nod and sometimes not. What I call the "American Express Negro"—meaning he's over here with a group of white people from the Midwest, Michigan or someplace —by and large *he* has not spoken. You know, he's with his white companions and they're *Americans* and it's "We are here and you are there!" I remember in Berlin a Negro friend and I went into a record store and this Negro girl was buying some records there. She appeared to be a student at the University of Berlin. She was with a white American fellow and she made every effort in the world to blind herself to the fact that there were two other American Negroes in the store. It was a very pointed "I-don't-know-you-don't-talk-to-me-don't-even-look-at-me" kind of thing, very, very obvious. It happens here in Rome, also.

I find that the older Negroes are more apt to speak than the younger Negroes. I was in New York in the summer of 1964 at the height of the riot in Harlem and I noticed that just generally in terms of the so-called Negro Revolution in New York, there was this kind of brotherly thing among

Negroes. Particularly after the riot, you would get on the subway train in the morning and all the Negroes began to kind of realize that they were part of the same team—that really impressed me before I left the States.

Why did it happen, this attitude? I think that the so-called Negro Revolution is beginning to take on the feeling of a real revolution. Instead of the what I call "NAACP compromise kind of attitude," which Negroes accepted before because some progress was being made, however small, people are beginning to express what they *really* feel, not biting their tongues as they did twenty years ago, and the revolution is beginning to take on an honest, realistic kind of tone. Some of the real feelings are beginning to manifest themselves.

A friend of mine, Al Hendricks, who used to work for the New York *Post* but left the States during the same week I did and lives in Tangier now—suggested Americans should institutionalize three days of rioting every year so that Negroes can get all of their anger out, like "This is our three days"; let 'em run wild, because Negroes need it. All of the internal frustrations, anger, bitterness, at themselves and society and everything, they'd release it in these kind of things. It's ridiculous to have the NAACP saying, "Everything is all right," because for the guy on 117th Street, that doesn't mean a damn thing. Or for the President to say, "Robert Weaver is now Chairman of the Housing and Urban Development"—what does that mean??? It doesn't mean anything to the guy on the street . . . believe me, all this talk about the "Negro middle-class." *Most Negroes are still poor!* And they are still living in the ghetto and that's it! Sure, there's a middle-class, but it's *small*. And the hatred is growing every day.

I've been over here eleven months and I've not written one word for the *Liberator*. I ask myself, "Why?" One reason is I don't hate white people, because there is a profound difference between the white American and the white European—in short, I have not been *angry*. Have I missed the tension? At times. Did it make any contribution to my art? Yes and no. It does something for your art insofar as it makes you kind of concern yourself with the whys and wherefores—you say, okay, *why* is there tension? In that respect, the tension has caused Negroes to examine themselves, examine their society and examine the relationship of themselves to that society.

I was fortunate to be able to get enough of the tension to continually investigate, to realize, for instance, why Europeans like jazz and respect jazz *as an art form* in a much more serious way than people do in America. A Negro spiritual to the average European is a great contribution to the musical culture of the world. I don't think you find this in America. Many Negroes themselves—the emergent Negro middle-class, to get back to *them* again—divorce themselves from jazz and Negro spirituals and Negro culture as such. I've noticed also with the emergence of a Godfrey Cambridge as a comedian—a Dick Gregory—a Bill Cosby—there is a return, but it's a return in many cases that has come from the *white* culture; *they* have put *their* stamp of approval on it first, then the Negro has picked it up, instead of the Negro picking it up first.

There is a problem that I'm going to face, too. I'm rapidly falling into that same category of being the expatriate Negro in a white community, a white European community, where color doesn't have that much to do with one's existence and, in a sense, forgetting The Problem. Yet it's the kind of thing I realize that I *must* always be aware of, be kept abreast of, because when you go back to America you find it hard to adjust to what's going on and, let's face it, America is my home. I haven't given up America. So I feel I have to be aware of what's going on. In the year I've been here, there have been changes. Too many of the Negroes I've met here have been away too long, their thinking is old-fashioned.

Europeans are sometimes as eager to like or accept Negroes, seeing them as symbols, perhaps, as white Americans are not to know them. In Scandinavia, from what I hear, this is exactly the case. They tell me you go there and they follow you down the street—I have not been there but I will go—and I have been told by whites that it's bad for the Negro because it puts him on the opposite end, rather than being hated he's loved so much that he's loved into madness. *I* say this: *every* Negro in America should have this for a while because he's been "put down" so long; let him have the big, tall, Anita Ekberg blond white girls chasing him down the street. He *needs* it! He may not need it for his entire life but I think the change would do him good!

Some of the Folk Studio people and I did a concert here in Bologna. The title of the show was the *International Songs of Rebellion,* and we, as American Negroes, were called in because of the Negro "revolution." *Before* we came out on stage and *before* we even opened our mouths, there was a standing ovation for four minutes! And, you know, it bugged me, because when we opened our mouths we could have been the two worst singers in the world and it would have been a drag. I want to be *good* and I want to be accepted on my own merit, rather than as a symbol of the oppressed masses. But yet, and still, I said to myself, "Well, damn. I'll accept it. And I will work that much harder to be that much better."

Has the Mussolini experience left its heritage in racist feelings here? No. When I came here, I thought it would be like in Germany, where you could never seem to get rid of the feeling that this was the enemy, this was the home of

Naziism, where six million people were put in the ovens and killed. But in Italy there's no legacy of the war at all because the Italians, by and large, didn't fight. The Italian soldiers are the worst in the world. Actually, they are the best soldiers but they never fight. They're just a beautiful people, Fascism meant nothing here. The partisans, the Resistance, was perhaps greater here than in any other country except France. I can see why, because the Italians are not a warlike people, they're a very peaceful people. and the soldiers are almost ridiculously funny.

Sicily and the major part of Italy are two different cultures. The Sicilian is considered almost as an American Negro was in America ten, fifteen years ago. Sicilians are darker, the illiteracy down there is quite high, and there are slums. Romans talk about "Sicilians and their knives" the same way a white American talks about Negroes carrying knives. Talk to a Roman or a Milanese about Sicily and *it's the same feeling,* that of the outsider and the insider, the Negro and the white American. Very strange. They don't mention it here. When they do bring it up it's "Oh, well, Sicily will take care of itself," you know.